DEEP SEAS
AND *Tall Ships*

DEEP SEAS
AND *Tall Ships*

A 21st CENTURY SEAMAN'S ACCOUNT OF
A LIFETIME OF DEEP OCEAN VOYAGES

PETER J. HILL

BA (HONS); MCA Chief Mate (Rtd)

Member: Royal Institute of Navigation

Peter Hill

2023

BREWIN BOOKS

BREWIN BOOKS
19 Enfield Ind. Estate,
Redditch,
Worcestershire,
B97 6BY
www.brewinbooks.com

Published by Brewin Books 2023

A CIP catalogue record for this book is
available from the British Library.

ISBN: 978-1-85858-757-8

Printed and bound in Great Britain
by Halstan & Co. Ltd.

Contents

Acknowledgements

Cover design:
Detailed design by Janette Hill *www.janettehill.com*

Cover photograph:
Tall Ship *Prince William* by Julia Brenchley: email *Tallshipmemories@live.co.uk*

Other photographs and artwork:
Page 5   Whistling lesson: photo by the late Isobel Warner
Page 13   Bridley Moor Senior School photo
Page 39   Author's artwork
Page 47   Changing weather: author's artwork and photograph
Page 55   HILL SIBLINGS watercolour by Janette Hill circa 1980
Page 57   Tall Ship image courtesy of Julia Brenchley (email above)
Page 80   Tall Ship image courtesy of Julia Brenchley (email above)
Page 94   Schooner MALCOLM MILLER image courtesy Jo Gauthier
            (*gauthiermarines.com*)
Page 101   Tall Ship image courtesy of Julia Brenchley (email above)
Page 104   Author's artwork
Page 109   Author's artwork
Page 116   Bombing of RFA SIR GALAHAD Falklands 1982: author's artwork

Author's footnote:
Other photos/artwork are from the Hill Family Photo Collection and the Author's personal collection of Tall Ship (and earlier seafaring) images/artwork, including photographs freely shared by other members of crew 1963–2015.

With thanks to all who voyaged beyond the sight of land – capturing the visual moments.

Dedication

To my wife Elaine; to our children: Brian, Brent, and Janette; and to our grand-children: Isaac, Elliot, and Maddison.

    For whom my lifetime story is told – An Ode written with love...

I will tell of ocean voyages
To engage the loving hearts
Of my dear children;
And enrich the lifetime journey
Of grandchildren living out their youthful years.
Memories of far-ocean mornings
And the deepest fathomed echoes of the sea.

I recall my years of childhood
And the comfort of
My early family fireside;
And the peaceful Indian Ocean
And the challenging
Adventures of my youth.

My storyline embraces
All the whispers and the power
Of the wind-song;
The lonely Southern Seaways
And the flight of albatross upon the wing.
Memories of far-ocean mornings
And the deepest fathomed wonders of the sea.
Precious years I spent in childhood
And the memory of
My warming cottage fireside;
To the wide Pacific Ocean
And the joyful homeward
Voyages of my life.

From those distant years of childhood
And the comfort of
My glowing family fireside;
To the grey Atlantic Ocean
And my recent homeward
Voyages under sail.
Memories of bright stars of evening
And the many ocean voyages of my heart.
Peter John Hill (Grandad), October 2022.

A footnote for my grandchildren: My experience of life has taught me to seek to prevail in the vast array of lifetime challenges; however, we must learn that triumph is not everything. Therefore, always strive to emerge as a winner; but when you fail, remember to learn from any experience of defeat. We cannot win every battle in life. But never stop learning. Never give up hope or compassion. Fight the good fight. Stay safe; and remember the kindness of strangers. Trust in the Good Lord. So, to my dear grandchildren – young and strong, richer than the summer skies: may your voices sing forever; may your morning songs be never silenced as the years go by.
Grandad Peter, 2023.

Introduction

My account starts at the age of two. Early dark days and some setbacks led to my determination to press on. At sea I learned to wonder: 'They that go down to the sea in ships… see the works of the Lord'. Psalm 107.

I have three trusted anchors: My close family; plus, lifetime seafaring (beginning as a young Cadet Officer in the UK's Merchant Navy); plus, life-affirming Christian values. As a 16-year-old, I exchanged my school uniform for my seaman's kit. My first voyages as a school leaver embraced winter Arctic waters to the wild Southern Latitudes. An early taste for seafaring adventure, with never a dull moment for a youthful seaman! (My 17th and 18th birthdays serving in my first ship). A young man's ocean life – wild-rovers all. Not one woman joined us during those first 14 months at sea. Not even a Captain's wife or daughter appeared to brighten our sea horizon. That's how it was in my youth. Arctic waters soon behind us, we left European seas astern via the Suez Canal. Onwards to Western Australia, South Australia, and New Zealand; later came orders for Durban and Bombay. Looking back, I took pen to paper many years after a 1963 sea passage from Western Australia to Durban. Aged 17, I observed in those wild southern seas a giant albatross flying above the mighty waves. That lone albatross was a symbol of our fragile humanity. The heroic endurance of that seabird, the grey-winged ghost, left a lasting impression of strength on my young seafaring mind.

Flight of the Grey-Winged Ghost (Observed in 1963: Fremantle to Durban)
Grey broad-winged pilgrim of this restless ocean
What sights embrace your gale-embattled flight?
Wild navigating seabird; born to windswept motion;
Over awesome raging seas of massive height.
What drives you onward with such lonely grace?
Who powers the energetic pulse within?
Can you endure this bleak forsaken place?
Your bold sea-days inspire my kith and kin.
Grey seabird of this Southern Wilderness;
How many gales have raised your sculptured span?
Seafaring myths are daily life to you.
How many storms have bruised your ancient clan?
Peter John Hill, 1997.

Looking back, I have my own story of life-endurance to tell. Enjoying the best of both worlds can be nothing more than a day-dream. But, for me, the concept of professional work both at sea and ashore has been a lifetime reality. As a child I experienced hard knocks. My father walked away when I was just five; as a result, I wanted to be around for my own children at key times. It worked for me. My early experience at sea led to responsibility ashore, with the ability to return to seafaring throughout life. But all choices involve a real cost: I did not take up an offer of career progression to a Master Mariner's 'ticket' in early life; and therefore, I did not progress beyond my final qualification as Chief Mate. However, I used my skills at sea into my 70th year. My compensating mid-life BA (Hons) degree opened up constant work ashore when I needed to be close to home and family. Overall, I answered the call of the sea throughout life. This resulted in challenging voyages – including a 25-year span of service in Tall Ships.

This account is an insight into the ocean's call and the freedom to follow the seafaring life in a wide range of ships. However, the story of my obscure early years begins in my grandfather's basic Worcestershire canalside cottage, at Spring Equinox, March 1946. Following my early childhood years, I was often on an emotional roller-coaster; but seafaring and my robust Christian faith would become the building blocks of my adult life. Often at junior school, I was in a dark place – a bruised child; later I became a sports-loving wild card. Seafaring began straight from senior school. And personal faith? Like the Christian writer C.S. Lewis in the 20th Century – I came to dwell in the 'Shadow of the Almighty' as an unpromising convert. I would then face many challenges as I began my new life at sea. Aged 16, *Amazing Grace* became my bedrock: my song for adult life.

During my final year in senior school, I recall feeling a genuine need for clear overall direction. In response to many searching questions at some long-gone schoolboy gathering, an Anglican Bishop suggested we should pray each day. He was being sincere. I took his advice; and the clear New Testament message of redemption flooded in and moulded my world view as I moved into adulthood. I came to understand the loving kindness of God. The 'Good Samaritan' and 'The Prodigal Son' became lifelong speaking subjects. When I left home to face the challenge of the sea in March 1963, I discovered both an adventurous life, plus the Good Lord as my stronghold. Overall, my regular seafaring lasted until the age of 69, and, during that time, I was never overtaken by any serious accident or disaster at sea. Most of my sea voyages were good voyages. Bad days were rare. My sea horizon was bright. My abiding memories are of ships, stormy seas and fellow sea-rovers. I therefore look back to March 1963, when, as a fresh-faced and very young seafarer, I began my journey into the unknown. I would endure long voyages in my youth, night watches, endless work on rolling decks, plus Christian fellowship and a welcome ashore in Europe, India, Australia, New Zealand and beyond. All in my first year of life in ocean-going ships. By the age of 20 years, I would serve as Officer of the Watch (OOW) in a newly built BP tanker voyaging East of Suez. Before my 21st birthday, I would be formally qualified as a UK deep-sea deck officer. New beginnings in every dimension of life.

All told, a far cry from my infant days in our cosy cottage beside a bleak canal, with my elderly Grandad Jack smoking his pipe and sawing his timber. Grandfather Jack Warner was my early rock, with my first five years of life lived out under his welcoming roof. My Grandfather, my housekeeping Aunt Isobel and my young mother provided my early shelter from the storms of life. Many storms were on my future radar, including some dark moments as a young child. I was never a victim in any way; but, the darkest days, as well as the good times, are the moments I must recall in this account as the following chapters unfold.

Enjoying the enduring peace established in Europe at the end of WW2, I would grow up and obtain an early start to my professional life in the Merchant Navy. I would marry and establish my own family home. I also witnessed historic moments in the modern world. Many changes took place. I watched on TV as Neil Armstrong took his first bold steps onto the Moon's surface in 1969. Shortly after that significant moment, I wrote my first serious words as a young poet. Years later I would meet up with a US astronaut on a sea passage from Darwin.

True Grit Lunar Landing 1969
Toward the distant stars
Bold lunar landing now proclaim;
We scratch the surface of the ice.
Profound fathoms of deepest blue remain.
While in our bitter, sordid world – eternal truth
Endures: Our Creator God is greater than
The stellar spheres of time and space.
Emmanuel; Divine Mercy; Amazing Grace.
Redeeming love is daily closer to us than
Our mellow-light companion
Our tide-embracing moon.
Peter John Hill, 1969.

Chapter 1

Seafaring Youth – The call of the deep oceans

Between 1963 and 2015 I answered the call of the deep oceans of the world. The raging storms and seductive calms haunt my memory as I recall this account at the age of 76. As I write, it is just a few years since completing my final professional sea voyage in my 70th year of life. I remain indebted to the fact that I continued to pass strict medicals for active sea-service, known to UK seafarers as the essential ENG1 examination. No medical. No Revalidation. No work. (The heavy smoking, heavy drinking, overweight UK seafarer of my early experience is becoming a relic of the past in the 21st Century). I have witnessed all the earth's oceans, in all their moods. My voyaging memories include North Atlantic summer storms, winter tempests, full-fury hurricanes, 30 metre high waves, glistening icebergs and bright Canadian mornings in the St Lawrence River. Add the different crews I have sailed with and the whole chronicle has left its deep stamp on my own life experience. I have witnessed Fijian crews catching large sharks from the stern of a cable ship in the Pacific Ocean. Shark fishing not for sport – but to preserve and serve at tables in their remote island homes.

My seafaring has included sombre days. I have known sailors commit suicide by jumping into the vast ocean at night, never to be found despite prolonged ship searches come daylight. As a young Cadet Officer, I was assigned the duty of sorting out and listing a pathetic handful of personal items, left behind by a very disturbed fellow seaman. I was young and alone, making notes in the cabin of a dead sailor. This kind of drama was a regular feature of my early years at sea. Old heads on young shoulders. A far cry from my carefree days at senior school.

Most of my lifetime sea memories are good memories. Joseph Conrad wrote of the joy of being young and at sea. For me, the joy spanned six decades of my life. I worked in roles ashore; but the wheelhouse of ocean-going ships has been one of the few places where I have experienced a sense of deep joy and complete satisfaction in any work role. Training for and taking on the role of Officer in Charge (OIC) of the ship's navigation watch, places duly qualified Merchant Navy men and women at the operational centre of their ship: the Officer of the Watch is the Captain's legal representative on the bridge, often in the middle of long stormy-night navigation routines, collision avoidance and general ship safety. Operational awareness and collision avoidance are all part of the job of the duty OOW.

'Standing Orders' on the bridge require the OOW to 'Call the Captain' in good time, should navigational doubts arise. Duty at sea requires confidence to be shown by every officer and a sense of trust between officers of all ranks. Collisions at sea, ship fires, groundings and the like can turn into full-blown marine disasters. Incidents can have simple, routine beginnings. Remember the *Titanic*; the *Herald of Free Enterprise*; and the daylight bombing of RFA *Sir Galahad* in the Falklands.

Responsibility comes early to the typical OOW. At age 20, I qualified as Second Mate (Foreign Going). A seasoned Second Mate is the ship's primary navigating officer and takes responsibility for the ship during the midnight hours when the Captain and other officers are asleep. This could be a tanker carrying 350,000 tonnes of oil between the Gulf States and Europe, or a mega-size container ship sailing through Pacific Ocean storms. The Merchant Navy world is full of interest, including tankers, container ships, auxiliary military vessels, cable-laying ships, research ships, island ferries, ocean liners and sail training vessels. I have been privileged to sail as OOW in many of these different types and class of ship. But sailors are often a strong taciturn breed, whatever class of ship they serve.

The restless sea will always challenge the sturdiest ships and crews. In my final years at sea to 2015, I spent many voyages as Navigator/OOW in UK sail training vessels. My role as an officer in training ships was very rewarding – with normal responsibility for taking the ship through the darkest hours of every night at sea, when most of the 60 souls embarked were below decks. I was trusted with the Navigator's role, plus major firefighting duties, crew supervision aloft and general safety management to the last day of my active sea-service. Aged 69, I disembarked in 2015 after my final Tall Ship voyage – with a broad smile and my sea-chest full of memories. But, no disasters ever on my watch. Thankfully.

Unlike many truly heroic members of the UK's military fraternity, no-one has every fired a shot at me in conflict. However, from time to time, in any seafarer's experience, the ocean throws its full force at those of us who venture beyond the sight of land. Therefore, my long association with ships has left a high level of salt-stained awe in my mind. I recall the crews, the ships, the voyages, the loneliness, the storms and the homecomings. I once reflected, after a winter Atlantic voyage, that the smiles of my children were brighter than the northern starry night. Family life was ever sweet. My own account before the reader has the taste of the sea's tempestuous nature: in my narrative, my photographs and my seafaring verse. The ocean leaves its own mark. From Thomas Hardy's romantic description, 'The sea breaths brine from its strange straight line', to my memory of the grey mountains of Arctic Norway, the calm of the Indian Ocean, and the company of a wandering albatross in the roaring southern seas.

I was captivated by my first long voyages as a seaman straight from school: almost fourteen months of endless sea-time – serving as a 'First Tripper' in *British Cormorant,* a new 16,000 dwt BP Tanker Company fleet vessel, voyaging from Arctic Norway to the remote wilderness of the southern seas. The UK's Merchant Naval fleet does everything at sea not covered by the Royal Navy. Therefore, for me, as a lifetime professional mariner, sea-duty would eventually mean my service in many types of seagoing vessel, including my much-loved sail training ships from 1989 onwards. This splendid squadron of ships forms the backbone of my story. Although my lifetime regret is that I did not study for my UK Master's Certificate when the opportunity was offered to me as a young officer, I was pleased when the UK MCA finally awarded my certificate as Chief Mate; this followed my series of winter Arctic voyages with the RFA (Royal Fleet Auxiliary Service) in 2001. I owe many people a debt of gratitude – including one to the RFA and to those bleak winter voyages to the Norwegian Arctic.

Because I was privileged to serve my final years of regular sea-time as a deck officer in our fleet of UK Tall Ships, I reflect extensively in later pages on seafaring under sail. Sail training was an excellent way to end my days on the bridge of a ship. I enjoyed the personal satisfaction of serving as regular crew in seven UK sail training vessels from early 1989, including the world-famous schooner *Sir Winston Churchill*; plus, the renowned UK vessels, purpose-built for the disabled, the *Lord Nelson* and her wooden hulled sister ship *Tenacious.* Nautical science courses, good sea days, bad sea days, endless learning, regular medicals and ongoing revalidation of my UK MCA certificates are all part of this: my seaman's account, as laid down in these pages. I invite the reader to travel with me along the seaways of memory in this – my survival story from childhood.

Always, new technology found its regulatory way to the bridge of ships in which I served. From the traditional navigation skills learned in my youth voyages: PZX triangles, hour angles, azimuths and noon latitudes of my cadet training, to our postmodern sea-world of advanced radar systems, satnav and GMDSS (global distress comms at the press of a button). The electronic computer-enhanced kit on the bridge of our regular merchant ships is staggering in the 21st Century. However, seafarers don't change much. So, all human life is still afloat in every nautical mile of modern life at sea and in sea ports across the globe: the 21st Century fraternity of the sea. To this day, my own claim has remained the same; I have survived the technology changes and the regular hazards at sea by the grace of God and the kindness of strangers. Plus, regular support from many good-hearted seafaring men and women. And when youth had passed, regular support continued throughout from Elaine, my wife of over 50 years, and the supportive interest of my children and grandchildren. I have always made myself comfortable in hurricane force winds and in the comfort of my own fireside. I treasure the memory of both. Life has been a rewarding journey. No experience is ever wasted. Even difficult issues caused by childhood trauma can be dealt with, providing we find enough ways to rebuild lasting confidence and maturity.

So, let my sea narrative unfold with my vivid memories of childhood. I will recall halcyon days; also, some very grey shadows. Life can teach us to endure difficult struggles. The term Southern Ocean does not appear in my *Times Atlas of the World*, or in Admiral Smyth's *Sailor's Word Book*. But it is a real region at around latitude 50 degrees south of the Equator. Its brutal force exists. I have sailed very close to Southern Ocean storms, which run parallel to my worst experiences of life. We can all learn from the strength of a wandering albatross, and that seabird's struggles in those vast southern seas. We all need to rise above the occasional cruel waves pounding our fragile lives: like that grey-feathered bird riding out the storms of my early ocean voyages. Overall, my refuge from age 16, has been the grace of God – plus the regular kindness of trustworthy strangers.

Seafaring Youth: My memory of yesterday

In sunburned youth we sailed the seven seas
A multitude of sights to greet our eyes;
The contrasts and the chaos of Bombay.
Watch-keeping nights – beneath the ancient skies.
New Zealand bound, behold the Southern Cross
And sail with albatross upon the wing.
The riches of the jewelled tropic night.
Pleiades, and the light that morning brings.
So, when our salt-stained youth was past and gone
And when life-duties called from distant shore
Haunted memory of the savage sea remained
The thunder of its vengeance, and its roar.
True sailors are a different breed of men;
We carry in our hearts the myriad rays
Of Aurora Borealis: wistful hopes
That sunburned youth returns in later days.
Peter John Hill, 1997.

Chapter 2

Childhood – Early links to the lonely seas

With my Grandfather Jack Warner: A whistling lesson in the sun, circa 1949.

I am a native of rural Bromsgrove, set in rolling English farmland. My cottage birthplace was an early link with a wider world: Gloucester, the Severn Estuary and the sea. With 1946 snow thick on the ground, I was born into the warm-hearted simplicity of the tied-cottage occupied by Grandad Jack Warner, on the side of the Worcester to Birmingham canal – as described in detail by Pat Warner, my late mother, in her own social history entitled *Lock Keeper's Daughter*, Brewin Books (1986). I never knew my maternal Grandmother Agnes; she died shortly after giving birth to my mother. (Premature death cast its darkest shadow over that Warner cottage). However, my vivid recollections of my first five years under my grandfather's roof are mostly cheerful memories. For me, the Warner darkness was to take hold from the age of five and follow me through to junior school days. Dear Grandfather Jack Warner was destined to die in 1952; and about that time, Thomas, my young father, finally walked away, as I shall recall. This bleak interlude left its lasting mark on my childhood days.

For the 1940s Warner family, life was cosy, but far from easy in that Canal Company cottage, with no running water and no electrical power until 1951. Fresh water was carried in buckets, drawn from the wells of the home of neighbour and local historian George Bate. My unmarried Aunt Isobel (Bib) Warner ran my early cottage home. She had a fearsome reputation; but I always found her kind and welcoming. I spent more time with Aunt Isobel than with my nurse-in-training mother during my first five years of life. It was a very primitive lifestyle, but I remember the books, a radio and an ancient telephone; and the changing canal life passing by, in the form of working narrow boats and wildlife. By way of contrast, I well remember in my early 60s, walking around a lighthouse keeper's family cottage in North America dating from 1910, with its museum preserved lighting, kitchen, bathroom and central heating. The US lighthouse keepers and their kith and kin, seemed light-years ahead of the late 1940s Brits. The 'Land of the Free' developed some very appealing benefits.

Our canalside cottage home looked snug enough in Aunt Isobel's Kodak box-camera photographs. As an infant, I can recall gangs of men rope-hauling barges and scenes of ice-breaking vessels on the frozen canal. This bleak mid-winter outlook was punctuated by warm summer days. We had the large Cadbury fishing Reservoir as a backyard and the dripping Lock Number 53, part of the famous Tardebigge Flight, at the towpath frontage. My Grandfather always kept his pigs close to the cottage. Many bitter tears from distant family days lingered about the place. The cottage had seen the full drama of life and death as it touched the Warner family from the 1920s. A history of very tragic loss of life.

My Grandfather was 72 when he died. He had worked day and night until his retirement; and he had witnessed many tragic heartache moments according to my mother's book. She paid tribute to the courage of her down-to-earth father. Grandad Jack Warner had endured many years of faithful toil, but died leaving only memories – after a lifetime of skilled labour and his regular tears; but he often found the strength to sing. He was renowned for his ballads and songs during drinking sessions at the Halfway Public House. My mother recalled his voice across the years singing, *My World Forever, the Sunshine of your Smile.*

I remember Jack Warner as a kind, quiet and patient man. But my grandfather carried his burden of sorrows. He had witnessed the premature death of five of his seven children. Grandmother Agnes Warner, well into middle-age, gave birth to my mother and died three years later. My late mother, Patricia Violet Warner, recalled her own early youth in Reservoir Cottage. She recalls in her first book,

My father looked so old and weary. There were times in his life when he was utterly bewildered as to why fate had been so unkind to him, after the early happy days of his marriage. Family sorrows were never discussed; but at certain times my father looked so broken with grief and loss. Our 1930s/1940s cottage home was filled with evidence of his sorrows. Little treasures and trinkets tucked away in boxes and drawers: a hair slide, a faded photograph, a hymn book, a neatly folded embroidered handkerchief.

My late mother relates going back to the banks of her childhood reservoir playground, but she could not face walking to look again at her deep-joy-and-sadness family cottage – the late Jack Warner's home beside Lock Number 53. Warner family life seemed like history lived out on a roller-coaster. My mother remained a Warner at heart until her dying day. My own raw emotional roller-coaster would commence after my 5th birthday, soon after the death of Grandad Jack and the departure of my father.

The story of my early childhood, sketched out above, begins with my earliest memory as a very young boy in our canalside home. I have family memories from the age of two, plus a handful of recollections of a hardworking, young mother married to my rarely seen-at-home young father. Their early marriage was destined to fail; but my late mother remained a closed book on the subject throughout her long life. I was the aftermath of her own early experience with marital reality. I can recall Thomas, my unemployed young father. Twice he took me swimming; once he pointed to a Spitfire flying overhead. That is about all I can recall of any real interaction between father and infant son, except my attempts to separate my parents during their bitter arguments. No surprise that their marriage quickly ended as the economic and social reality of the post-WW2 years began to unfold. I have often reflected on their short-lived marriage. (I was aware as a child of very long divorce proceedings, discussed in hush-hush tones, in conversations between my mother and her sister Isobel).

Overall, there was little work, no money and limited 1950s prospects. My mother was a young trainee nurse, drifting on hope with a young son. But there was one bright moment amidst the turmoil just before I started infant school in 1951: my mother was handed the keys to a newly-built semi-detached council house with three bedrooms and 1950s mod-cons. Plus, the biggest garden you could ever want. My mother deserved a few days of good fortune. They came in the shape of those keys to a brand-new front door – part of the post-war boom-time housing development in the UK. A white painted house, on the Bromsgrove side of a hard-drinking, needle-making town called Redditch. After five years of cheerful isolation in and around a canal cottage, surrounded by wildlife, canal folk and water, I was suddenly confronted with loud baby-boom children yelling and screaming in urban life. All the wild playmates you could ever want. Plus a few you didn't need. Many a childhood skirmish would break out. From the age of five years, I would learn the art of survival in a very different world. Muddy canal and narrow boats – on to many cuts and bruises. Early endurance lessons.

However, the 1950s was an upbeat decade. It was to bring material benefits after the 1951 Festival of Britain and our new Elizabethan era. We enjoyed a big street party on that rainy Coronation Day in June 1953, and I would find myself watching the parade on a very small monochrome TV. Children could acquire a money box in the shape of a gilded coach. The 1950s was a time of bright simplicity after the nationwide social disruption of WW2. Looking back, popular writers like Andrew Marr seem to agree that WW2 changed life forever in the UK. I grew up a 1950s child in a decade of change. The UK also enjoyed fresh political leadership and the early days of the NHS, where my mother found permanent work as a trained junior nurse. In 1986, my mother would document her own life story referred to above in *Lock Keeper's Daughter* – written under her maiden name of Pat Warner. It went global. Fan mail from New Zealand.

In our new 1951 domestic surroundings of a council-built home, my restless young father Tom, for his own reasons, was a man constantly here today – gone tomorrow. During divorce proceedings, he seemed to appear from nowhere. This was unsettling for all concerned; and my divorcing parents had regular battles over money. Finally, my young father simply jumped ship. I recall letting him out onto a deserted street. I watched him leave the house wearing his army-surplus clothing. He did not look back. He just disappeared from my radar. I recall afterwards feeling great sadness as a child; and I was always fighting with my peers as a young boy. This blunt final departure left a deep scar that troubled me for years.

Later in life, after raising our own three children, I finally concluded that my dark moments, at that time, were further compounded by the sudden death of Grandad Jack Warner. The male role models in my life just seemed to vanish overnight. (In 1954, my mother would marry again and her difficult financial problems would end). My years aged 5 to 10 were a bit hit and miss to say the least. My choice of an early departure from home aged 16, to become a seafarer, would usher in a fresh start and a turning point, after my academic and sporting success at senior school. My seaman's life was destined to become a solace of freedom and independence during my early adult years. However, my junior years of regular chaos and emotionally raw days, would not provide an easy passage to maturity and self-confidence. I still had oceans to cross and mountains left to climb. Without a golden spoon to feed me, I would be off parental hands financially from my mid-teenage years. Aunt Isobel would leave me £300 in her will. The sea was destined to become a lifetime treasure trove.

When I look back, my junior days were spent on an unusual journey. Perhaps lifetime resilience is developed in this way? But I am fortunate not to have been marked for life by my dysfunctional family bonding and un-bonding. My mother's second marriage took place, with little ceremony, at a Registry Office around my eighth birthday – two or three years after her very long divorce. Second time round, she married a hardworking man: my well-meaning and often amiable stepfather Grosvenor Hill (just 'Grove' to his pals). He enjoyed 1950s socialising. Following National Service in the Royal Navy, he relished any bar-stool banter. He was a self-confessed loner in his youth, with a bright mind. He was also a car owner with local Black Country roots. He sported a sarcastic wit and a lifetime taste for horses; but he was smart with his bets and he rarely lost money. As a former Austin Motor Company apprentice, he was well paid as a supervising AMC foundryman when they married. Later, he also ran a Saturday market stall selling clothing. He liked to spend his money on shoes. It was also obvious that he was unsure of himself around a growing stepson. Unusual days for everyone. I began to call him dad. He came full of Black Country promise.

It was hard going at first. After the wedding, there were normal domestic issues to sort out. It is never easy walking into a ready-made family. Angry words would be exchanged. At times, the Warner in me was called on to respond to difficult episodes. Thankfully, not too much collateral damage in the long term. My regular escape became junior school; plus, later cycling my daily 12-mile return school-run. This would prove to be a great refuge in my final junior school days. From the age of 10 years, I was covering 60 miles a week in all weathers, to and from Stourbridge Road School in Bromsgrove. This daily return journey in itself developed a strong sense of real independence at an early age. I was hit by a speeding car on one home run; bike damaged – but I was uninjured. I did not report the incident at home. I was growing up fast, with a bent pedal trophy from the cars impact. The young male driver was shocked; he quickly fled the scene, speeding away from the mounted pavement after the collision. 1950s childhood memories. The joys of growing up can sometimes be limited.

My stepfather and I embraced toleration – in a patchy kind of way. As a 10-year-old, he began to take me to the cinema for company. Because it was always the last show, I would normally arrive late for school, after registration on the morning following. An unusual lifestyle? I simply had a different kind of family. My birth surname was forever a subject out of bounds, even with my mother. In 1954, my surname was therefore legally changed to Hill by formal Deed Poll. The general consensus was, 'You must learn to cope with your new name'. So be it. Somehow, we all survived. Never adopted, my stepfather allegedly referred to me as his 'Achilles heel' to some of his friends. But overall, he had several strengths. Soon there were three children, with the arrival of Karen and David. This band of siblings mostly got on well enough, as together we developed and muddled onwards. We remained close throughout our adult lives. Life would deliver, to each of us, its own patchwork of real problems to sort out as time rolled onwards. Best to dwell on the positive side of life. Sunny side up.

Looking back to those family days in the 1950s, I am reminded that we all had failings. Those distant days were hard and very basic; families no doubt did their best. Our home life saw much needed financial stability. I came to see that my mother had overcome many setbacks in life. I can recall her in her prime: as a busy nurse, caring for patients; and later in life milking her goats. As a father myself, I eventually came to view my stepdad as a man moulded by his own childhood home – which to me resembled a cold-comfort farm (but his parents always gave me a warm welcome). Overall, my stepdad enjoyed wood-turning, horses, malt whiskey and politics. To his credit, he mellowed with time; and in retirement he was very kind to my wife Elaine and to our daughter Janette. This long-overdue warmth marked a healing period towards the end of his days. Despite a few dark moments, life once more began to smile on me from the age of 10 onwards; by then I was thriving at junior school, as the next chapter will reveal. I learned to cope with the hazards of life; and I even survived the sarcastic wit at home. I would finally discover that breaking out of my own childhood mould would become very liberating. In the long term, the sea became my alma mater. The poets I quote have all supported my education in the school of life,

And so, I live you see;
Go through the world
Try, prove, reject, prefer
Still struggling to affect my warfare
Happy that I can be crossed and thwarted as a man
Not left in God's contempt apart
With… smooth life dead at heart:
Tame in earth's paddock as her prize.
Robert Browning

I often recall that 1963 grey-winged ghost of an albatross, gliding over the killer waves of the southern seas, finding strength to rise above the deadly storms.

Footnote: My mother loved my own three children: Brian, Brent and Janette. She was also delighted by the arrival of her three great-grandchildren: Isaac, Elliot and Maddison. My mother passed away when they were very young. My own story of endurance is just beginning, spurred onwards by early survival.

Photographs from my early childhood, (from the author's collection).

Left: Mother: Patricia Warner (her family surname). Nurse Pat Hill following her second marriage. Middle: My father: Thomas (Tom jumped ship in 1951). Right: Author: 1951 age 5, an unhappy school starter. Early loss of father and grandfather. My surname change caused a problem for teachers.

Chapter 3

Infant Schooldays Start – A chronicle of wasted time?

My first home for five years had been the secure retreat of my grandfather's cottage; age 5 to 10 – I was battered and bruised by family trauma; from 10 to 16 years, I finally gained confidence at school as an athlete, in my studies and later, as Head Prefect. My active youth was destined to be finally moulded by the wintry-fever of adventures at sea. After a slow start, I found school rewarding.

I spent my school days from age 5 to 11 at Stourbridge Road Infant and Junior School, Bromsgrove (Head Teachers: Miss Flat and Mr Abel). We lived 6 miles to the north during this entire period, and I cycled each day from age 10, as related above. Looking back, I disliked infant school, but enjoyed my junior school – although disturbed at times by the aftermath of the changes within my family. (In 1954, some school teachers would not acknowledge my new surname. Steep learning curve). Infant school just passed me by, although certain things remain vivid, 'Does he like milk?' There would be oceans of it – under the free school milk regime. We were tasked to collect the foil bottle tops as part of a national campaign. First day at school, aged 5 – the first question in my schooling concerned milk. Soon to be followed by endless rote-learning of times-tables.

Early reading? Familiar with books from the Reservoir Cottage days, I do not recall any struggle with reading. We also sang at frequent intervals: 'The big ship sails on the Ally-Ally-O'. Something to do with my future? Then there was the introduction to rank and power. Miss Flat, Head of Infant School, was very small and very stern. Had she been born with a look that could haunt schoolchildren for years? She would lecture us all about our many wild playground misdeeds: things that occurred once we got bored with 'Cops and Robbers'. She was an impressive four-foot female with a menacing cane. Our most severe crimes were worthy of The Tower of London. 'Someone has been tripping up children on the school field. Such behaviour will stop. Is that clear?' Miss Flat had that mean tone in her voice as she paced up and down. Call the local bobby? I was one of the tall lads standing at the back. We all shivered in our infant boots, before laughing it off. For my part, I can't say I enjoyed the infant regime of Miss Flat.

Once in junior school next door, my confidence grew. In academic testing, junior school reports placed me top-of-the-class for the last three years of school life to the age of 11 years. I even played school football for the B Team. I became physically strong – aided by the fact that throughout the final period of my junior school days, I cycled those 60 miles every week: travelling from home to school and back, often in the rain and snow. I also recall right at the end of my junior school days, enjoying a one-to-one high-jump competition, on the junior school playing field surrounded by the whole school of yelling Bromsgrove children. It was a Bromsgrove school; and I was the lone Redditch-based boy pitched against a local lad – my pal, Malcolm Bithell, who won the day by a small margin. Those days marked the start of my athletic strength and self-confidence. When cycling as a 10-year-old, I recall testing my roadside puncture repairs for leaks – by dipping the repaired innertube into murky rain-puddles. In the winter, it was snow and ice for weeks on end. Again, I managed to survive the cycling, the weather, better high-jumpers and the general survival demands of junior school life. And, sea air was drawing me nearer to the depths of the Ally-Ally O.

Despite 11+ exam failure in summer 1957, my life in the future of senior school was to be on an upward path. In July 1957, it was farewell to junior school, and a final farewell to my last junior school teacher, Mrs Tomlinson, who frequently showed an odd disapproval for my growing confidence, but nevertheless rated me as top-of-the-class in final tests. My junior school Head Teacher, Mr Abel, simply noted, 'Well done'. I rode off into the bright morning of HMG policy: secondary modern education. However, my senior school years were to be dominated by my active membership of teams and general success: Boy Scout patrols (I would lead the Hawk Patrol); demanding senior scout expeditions to Éire, Scotland and winter Snowdonia; senior school drama performances and scouting 'Gang Shows'; first Team football and cricket; County level swimming and athletics; senior school athletic records; RLSS Bronze Medal and Bronze Cross awards; Head Prefect leadership and public

Head Boy: Bridley Moor School.

13

speaking demands. Finally, aged 16, with a handful of GCE passes, I began BP Deck Officer training at sea.

It was a regret not making the grade for the local grammar school. Nevertheless, secondary education would serve me well enough, thanks to a special group of excellent teachers and Saturday morning football, managed by teacher and coach, Alan Harrison. He would eventually award me a top school trophy: 'Athlete of the Year 1961'. This would lead to my appointment as Head Prefect.

Chapter 4

11+ Exam – Then the flourish set on youth

1957 – Christmas, 1962: For all my growing self-confidence and top-of-the-class junior school results, I managed to fail the controversial UK 11+ test. Like many who failed, I walked into the test with zero exam prep. By virtue of this divisive UK testing, many pupils were destined to mediocrity on the voyage of life. (Later, I realised that to encourage a pass at 11+, business and professional parents probably encouraged their junior state school offspring with private tuition). Whatever the social injustice of the UK 11+ system, there was a post-WW2 baby boom competing for limited grammar school places. I was labelled a 'failure', and duly placed in the top stream of Bridley Moor County Secondary School, Redditch in September 1957. This new survival challenge would lead to the sea.

A rough and tough school. Much rowdiness. Later in life, I came to see the Government's selection to fail at 11-years-of-age as unjust. But there is always hope and diverse routes to achievement. My gift, such as it is, has always been to try to turn adversity into a positive result. (It was to happen several times in my life). It is the albatross rising above the white toothed waves. 'Always bounce back', would become a lifetime mantra. My senior school Headmaster, W.H. Pulman, MA (Oxon), was a man of high intelligence and wit. He believed in giving motivated students fresh opportunity. He is remembered as a remarkable Head and provided great encouragement to me – appointing me as Head Boy in my final senior year. Ironically, I was destined to leave school at 16 with GCE 'O' level passes in 5 subjects, including English Language, maths and physics. This matched many a grammar school pupil of my generation leaving school at 16. However, I am aware that many 11+ failures of my day were marked for life. Our Careers Officer informed my own cohort that we would never rise above being construction site supervisors. This comment marked my path to political insight.

After several hit and miss years at infant and early junior school, I had toughened up mentally and physically. Alongside those emotional struggles from the age of five, I spent a lot of time in boyhood battles. I lost teeth along the way; in some of those long-gone conflicts I suffered the blows of bigger fists. By early senior school I was defending myself, standing my ground and making my mark. As a young sportsman and athlete, I was given a wide berth by most troublemakers; and I learned to deliver a hard punch when challenged. I had also taken a positive interest in maths and science before arrival at secondary school. Electricity had been an unknown luxury in my infant cottage home. However, I experimented with the lights and fuses in our new council house – and, at the age of eight, I managed to blow the main house fuse. Too much curiosity. Aunt Isobel had often used the term 'curiosity killed the cat', in answer to my frequent questions. The day I blew the main house fuse almost killed me. Saved by the main fuse. I was exploring and growing up fast. Camping trips, sport and good teachers were destined to become my stronghold as I moved through early secondary school years. I set my sight on grasping academic subjects.

There were many high points at senior school between 1957 and 1962. Some early lessons in leadership also. As mentioned above, I am indebted to a far-sighted Headmaster at Bridley Moor, who had appointed gifted teaching staff across a range of key academic areas; and on one occasion, brought in a renowned symphony orchestra to introduce his school to classical music (in the early days of English pop-star Billy Fury). Some of my own senior schoolboy achievements follow, but I will first relate an early lesson in leadership (aka – when the wheel comes off, it may be time to back down). The history goes something like this…

After my ongoing success in team sports, county level athletics and swimming, I was still surprised to become Head Boy in January 1962; I then decided overnight that the school was too rowdy and undisciplined between lessons. My team of prefects was destined to clear up the mess. I had the authority to sign detention notices. So, after my appointment to elevated high authority, I called a prefects' meeting and led from the front. I had noted a rousing battle speech by a Shakespearean actor at the cinema. It was now my opportunity to turn the tide. I would motivate my generals from my white horse, and lead the battle cry. Together, we would clean up the school. My tin-pot dictator speech won the day, resulting in a great and glorious rousing of true hearts of oak. We went into battle, and, very quickly, I learned an important lesson about true leadership: rhetoric is not the answer. Stirring speeches delivered to an inexperienced team can quickly make matters worse. My ill-judged words would lead to a strong negative reaction. In my case, climb-down was just a heartbeat away. This was to be a life-illuminating incident in my final year of preparation for sea-training.

My prefects went into action the morning after my rousing speech. Any misdeed in the school corridors resulted in a 'fixed penalty' note with my signature, authorising immediate after-school detention. Never had the school seen so many held back at day's end. There was worse to come in the form of well organised strong opposition from all pupil cohorts – lapel badges produced with the capital letters APO displayed: Anti-Prefect Organisation. Many staff were on my side, which was encouraging; but I can still see the Deputy Head as he passed me, disapprovingly shaking his head in total disbelief, as if to say, 'This is 1962, whatever are you doing?' I cannot recall that he ever spoke to me again. Within 24 hours, I quietly withdrew my fellow prefects and called the whole thing off. However, there were no reprisals; rank and file teachers seemed to forgive my headstrong ways. I learned a valuable lesson as I approached my 16th birthday. The Head was not critical in any way; and the APO lost impact as soon as my troops returned to barracks. I left the chaos in school corridors to police itself. Nobody ever got hurt, so I just got on with my sporting interests, school plays and non-confrontational speech making. We all learned from the train-smash exercise at Bridley Moor County Secondary School in the early spring of 1962.

My sports results at Bridley Moor – led me to 1962 Head Perfect status:
1st place: Junior Discus 1959
1st place: Junior Freestyle Swimming Relay 1959
1st place: Senior Discus 1961 (New school record)
2nd place: Senior Mile 1961
1st place: Senior Breaststroke 1961
1st place: Senior Discus 1962 (New school record)

Plus:
1960: Life Saving: RLSS Bronze Medal/1961 RLSS Bronze Cross
1961: 1st Eleven Football and 1st Eleven Cricket Teams
1961: Captain School Cross Country Squad
1961: School 'Athlete of the Year' Trophy
Jan 1962: Appointed Head Boy – based mainly on success in sport

Additional results: Redditch District Schools' Sport Competitions:
1961: 1st place: Senior Boys' Breaststroke (Local Senior Schools' Gala)
1961: 1st place: Senior Boys' Discus (Local Senior Schools' Sports Day)
1961: 3rd place: Senior Boys' Shot (Local Senior Schools' Sports Day)

Additional results: Worcestershire County Athletics and Swimming:
1961: Discus: Member of Worcestershire County Athletics Squad
1962: County Swimming Championships – 2nd place Senior Breaststroke

My senior scout expeditions to Éire, the Highlands of Scotland, and to winter Snowdonia were real physical challenges. Little wonder that I set my sights on an active sea-going career. My academic success at age 16 would provide me with 5

GCE 'O' level passes in maths, English Language, physics, geography and art. Success breeds confidence, and my youthful upbeat state of mind can be perceived in accounts included in the *Bridley Terminal* during my final years at senior school. In the December 1961 edition, I managed to get six separate mentions of my senior school success story. On the front 'cultural' page, I am mentioned as a regular 'bit-part-actor' in a production entitled *Listen to the Wind*; plus, a further five mentions in the sports section.

> First XI Soccer report, *Prominent in attack: P.J. Hill*; Senior House Soccer Matches, *First Place Saint David's House Team: Captain P.J. Hill*; Swimming Club: *Senior Boys' results outstanding: including P.J. Hill*; *Senior Boys Breast Stroke: 1st Place P.J. Hill*; *Royal Life Saving Society Bronze Cross: P.J. Hill*.

I do not claim to have been outstanding; I simply enjoyed every life-enhancing opportunity on offer at school and beyond.

Aged 16, I was beginning to produce reports of my UK expeditions. The following report on winter mountain training was included in the school *Bridley Terminal* in July 1962, entitled *Mountaineering in Snowdonia…*

> *During the last Christmas 1961 school holiday, former pupil Colin 'Greasy' Greer and I spent a week with thirty other Senior Scouts from all over the UK, exploring the mountains of North Wales. Our HQ was the Youth Hostel at Capel Curig. It was cold; it was bleak. It was Base Camp: Heinz 'Sandwich Spread' for a week.*
>
> *No time was lost getting down to work. Our first full exploration day was spent on snow-covered Moel Siabod. The mountains of North Wales were under Arctic conditions for the whole week. This was a far cry from school.*
>
> *Time passed quickly. We spent days engaged in rock climbing, mountain walking and navigation; there were lectures in mountain rescue. It was soon time for a full two-day exercise on Snowdon. The ultimate aim was to place an overnight camp on or near the summit. The exercise was carried out under difficult climbing conditions, with deep drifting snow and the menace of ice. Although the conditions were testing, and the overnight camp near the summit bitterly cold, it was a most enjoyable and exciting time. It is a moving experience to stand on the highest point in England and Wales, high above the clouds, and watch the sun rise on a cold, white world.*
>
> Peter John Hill, 5/1, 1962 *The Call of the Wild Sea Beckons.*

Chapter 5

Schooldays End – To learn the seaman's art and scope

In the autumn term of 1962, (I had opted for a one-term return to re-sit GCE maths and English), I was returning on a train from London following a successful interview with BP (aka British Tankers), and the offer of a three-year period of sea-training, spread over four years, to serve as a BP deck officer. I had visited a smart London office in BP's Britannic House, feeling well outside of my provincial comfort zone. I had no real idea what I was signing up to. My mother and stepfather thought I was joining something akin to the Royal Navy. A summary of my signed and sealed Indentures can be found below. I was to be provided with intensive sea-training and a small average income of £220 a year. (I concluded later on that nobody in my family noticed the low training pay). The terms apprentice and cadet were being merged in the 1960s. I would be treated as a Cadet Officer in training, to qualify as Second Mate (FG) – the first step to becoming a Master Mariner. With a company of high repute and a long history, as BP was, this was a step in the right direction. But I was 16, with no idea that I would begin my sea-going adventure by spending almost 14 months away in my first ship. I was destined to voyage from Arctic seas to southern storms before my 18th birthday. A very long way from my Head Boy speeches and Saturday football.

My early voyages with BP brought me face-to-face with the important survival lesson demonstrated by a wandering albatross in the southern seas: learn to rise above the angry storms. Many 11+ failures, with challenging family histories, were destined to mediocrity. But there was no need ever to feel like an outcast, even though HMG policy was aimed at secondary mods churning out lowly results: industrial fodder rewarded with small pay packets: life on a production line. The awesome sea took some of us to its bosom. Positive attitude plus opportunity are strong winning features. I would eventually study Prof John Adair: Action Centred Leadership. We all need to find an open-door offering training stimulus. BP opened the door to life across the oceans of the world.

To recap on my BP interview: Before joining my first ship as a 16-year-old boy, I was required to visit the London HQ of the BP Tanker Company, dressed for the occasion in my best suit, to be interviewed by the senior training Captain. As indicated, I passed this autumn 1962 interview, subject to finally gaining maths and English Language passes at GCE 'O' level. The training Captain was mainly impressed with my RLSS Bronze Cross for lifesaving and my all-round sports record. My vision was also tested for colour blindness. I was impressed by BP and its fleet of ships. Teachers at school were also impressed. In reality, I owed each one of them a debt of real gratitude. Alan Harrison for sport; Fred Kemp for maths; Bill Wear for English; Stan Johnson for physics; Steve Saunders for swimming and life-saving; plummy Mrs Court-Hampton for geography; Dudley Fowkes for music; Pete Williams for woodwork; and many more dedicated staff.

In 1963, I paid for my BP uniform and start-up kit, plus all nautical science books. I used a bank loan of £100. This I paid back over a two-year period out of my monthly 'allotment' of £9, leaving me £2 a month 'in the ship'. Cometh the big spender! The BP tanker fleet was all set to become a life changing experience of early worldwide travel, long periods away from home and early emotional independence. The following personal photographs indicate the great leap forward awaiting me after my worthwhile active days in senior school. Moving on from lifesaving to life-changing sea-service at 16. All about new survival skills.

Left: 1964: A fresh-faced young BP Cadet Officer.
Right: 1966: As a 20-year-old officer with BP.

Footnote: Appointed OOW in tanker *British Kestrel* in 1966. I was appointed by Captain Freeman during the last few months of my sea-training. We were voyaging from the UK, travelling East of Suez. It was a life-changing voyage, using all the knowledge and skills I had acquired at sea. During a challenging sea transit of the Straits of Messina, the Captain joined my Bridge Team on duty.

Early seafaring moments from 1963: all before reaching my 18th birthday.

British Cormorant: We enter Venice, 1963.

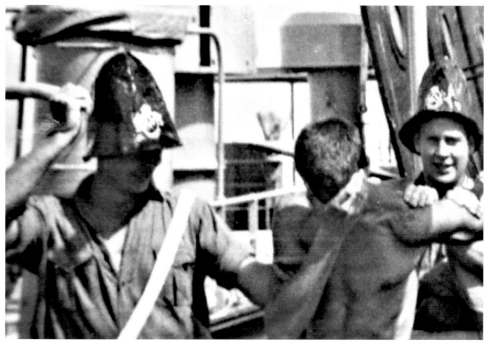

Crossing the Line: Neptune's Squad, 1963.

British Cormorant: Sydney Harbour, 1963.

Before proceeding to my first ship, I signed my very detailed BP Tanker Company Indentures. A Cadet Officer would sign Indentures as an Apprentice, a traditional Merchant Navy term in use long before the 1960s, placing responsibility both on the cadet and the shipping company. It was a binding 'contract' – sealed with the BP Tanker Company seal; and signed and witnessed by all parties, including a parent or legal guardian of the young Indentured seafarer.

The Indenture document was a long legal parchment document; therefore, highlights as follows will indicate the solemn formality and low training pay.

*THIS INDENTURE made 28th February 1963… between **Peter John Hill**… of the first part, and BP Tanker Company Limited, London of the second part… and Grosvenor Lyndon Hill (herein called the Surety) of the third part… WITNESSETH, That the said **Peter John Hill** hereby voluntarily binds himself Apprentice to the said company… for the term of FOUR years, from the date hereof; and the said Apprentice hereby covenants that, during such time, the said Apprentice will faithfully serve the said company, and obey the lawful commands, both of the said company and of all officers of any vessel on board of which he may be serving under this Indenture, and that the said Apprentice will not absent himself* *from their service without leave; IN CONSIDERATION WHEREOF… the said company hereby covenants with the said Apprentice, that during the said term… they will and shall… teach him… to perform the duties of a deck officer, and provide the said Apprentice with sufficient meat, drink, lodging… medicine and medical support… surgical assistance…* **and pay the said Apprentice the sum of £854 (in total over a four year period)… together with a further sum of £30 payable after satisfactory service for the term of this Indenture… (plus) twelve shillings yearly in lieu of washing**… *the said Apprentice providing for himself all wearing apparel.* (n.b. **£220 average pay per year, with all living expenses paid).**

My Indentures were registered at the Mercantile Marine Office, Port of Tilbury, London on 28th February 1963: I was signed up – four years hard slog!

The final completed Indentures also record my 36 months of sea-time:

- Signed-On MV *British Cormorant* on 1st March 1963; Signed-Off 15th April 1964.
- Signed-On SS *British Comet* on 22 June 1964; Signed-Off 26th January 1965.
- Signed-On SS *British Signal* on 6th March 1965; Signed-Off 30th August 1965.
- BP then sent orders for me to join an advanced Nautical Science Course at South Shields for 3 months Sept–Dec 1965 (Counted as full sea-time). This excellent course for 27 cadet officers, resulted in my ranking as 3rd in overall academic performance, with an average of 73% in seven nautical subject areas, including Principles of Marine Navigation (87%) and maths (75%). The course under Captain D.M. 'Robbie' Robinson (Extra Master) transformed my understanding of the technical subjects underpinning the role of a deck officer in the 1960s Merchant Navy. It was an academic leap forward, providing me with a real confidence boost. Following this 3-month advanced course, my final training months at sea began. Sea-service as OOW was just around the corner for me.
- Signed-On MV *British Kestrel* on 2nd January 1966; appointed OOW during deployment.
- After my second BP sponsored period at South Shields Marine College from September 1966 – I qualified as Second Mate (FG): 6th January 1967 – passing all parts of the UK DTI examination at the first attempt. This single qualification inspired my sea-service for six decades of my life, and eventually provided an ongoing income to fund my BA (Honours) Degree in Combined Studies: 2.1, in middle life, (1984–1988).

Later, I qualified as a UK MCA Chief Mate on 18th September 2001. I served as a regular deck officer until the age of 69 years, ending my sea career serving as a Navigating Officer in seven UK sail training ships. During BP training at sea from March 1963 – to qualifying as Second Mate, in just under four years, I moved from schoolboy to manhood, and gained broad worldwide seafaring experience. Memorable voyages. Early responsibility is life-changing. A part-remembered poem from my schooldays comes allegedly from a native tribal North American warrior – name and tribe unknown; but the warrior muse is fitting for the seafaring mind. I have lost the original title, so I made up a label.

Ode to Endurance: Walk like a Warrior
Do you feel the bite of the storm?
The sting of the rain?
Face them; embrace them; be savage again;
Go hungry and cold like the wolf;
Go wade like the crane.
The palms of your hands will thicken
The skin on your face will tan –
Windswept, resolute, determined
You will also walk like a man.
Anon – perhaps old-fashioned in the 21st Century?

Further reflections: The transition from my senior school, with sporting and Head Boy status, to joining my first BP Tanker was quick and sharp. I did not attend 'sea-school' before joining my first ship; therefore initial embarkation was akin to landing on a different planet, with little knowledge of the language. I applaud BP as the organisation providing my seafaring foundation. As the years unfolded after my cadet years, I would take a living from the sea at some point during six rolling decades of my life. BP Tanker training in my youth was truly life enhancing. One of my deepest regrets therefore, was ditching my early BP sea career before my 21st birthday. As already indicated, upon completion of BP sea-training (and service as OOW while still in training) I was made the clear offer of a Third Officer contract by BP Tanker HQ staff in the summer of 1966. I was barely out of my teenage years, with no real experience of the financial realities of living. The offer was handed to me on a plate. And with all the wisdom of youth I turned it down. It was a bold choice I would live to regret. Therefore, six months after the offer, I walked away from BP with my hard-won UK Certificate of Competence as Second Mate (FG). In many ways, I then made myself an unnecessary hostage to fortune for some time. Career sense can be a long time coming.

We must all learn to value genuine people offering fleeting opportunities in life. I was fortunate enough to retain my seafaring skills for another day. In summary, in 1966, I walked away from my service with the BP fleet, and from the early financial security offered by BP as a leading UK ship owner. Sometimes youth can be far too headstrong. Nevertheless, the good memories of those BP training years remained bright and fresh in my mind: the excellent officers with whom I served; the excellent ships in which I served. However, for all my financial naivety, I remained mentally strong and confident; and I then faced an unknown but challenging future. Over time, I would discover new opportunities at sea. In my youth, I had never considered the magnificent sail training ships making a worldwide impact from the 1950s onwards. Little did I realise what a huge future impact these ships would have on my own professional life – as late as 1989 and beyond to 2015. Before returning to my many sea voyages, this is a moment to pause and reflect on the heart of John Masefield's *Sea Fever*.

I must go down to the seas again, to the lonely sea and the sky,
And all I ask is a tall ship and a star to steer her by,
And the wheel's kick and the winds song and the white sails shaking,
And a grey mist on the sea's face and a grey dawn breaking.
I must go down to the seas again, for the call of the running tide
Is a wild call and a clear call that may not be denied…
John Masefield

Tall Ship: The bow from the foremast yards. The author was supervising work aloft.

Chapter 6

Navigation – Learning something rich and strange

My 1963 BP sea-kit was obtained entirely at my own expense: ranging from a No. 1 black 'Doe-skin' uniform and cold weather great-coat to full tropical kit, black shiny shoes, white shoes, white shirts and navy blue working gear: the whole nine yards. Essential study books were expensive, including Charles Cotter: *The Elements of Navigation* and *Norrie's Tables*, plus *Admiralty Manuals of Seamanship*. I wondered what the working gear was all about, and was soon to find out. The glossy BP booklets showed officers and cadets relaxing in onboard comfort, dressed in white tropical uniforms. The reality for a 1960s officer cadet/apprentice involved endless hours of deck work – to gain a 'Seaman's Safety Eye'. The first twenty-four months focused on daily study plus tasks of practical seamanship and ship upkeep; the final period of 'serving your time' at sea would focus on advanced study, plus developing the skills of safe navigation and general duties of a competent officer. What did we see? We saw the sea. In all its moods, and across the world. We also got to view oil refineries all over the globe. Approaching tanker berths at all hours of day and night; sailing away from our home port on Christmas Eve; delayed at anchorages awaiting pilots. Oil refineries morning, noon and night. These were constructed miles from towns and cities. But I would always make time to explore ashore, and pay the cost of little or no 'flaking out' in port. So, I would work in port for eight hours on deck, go ashore for another eight hours, return to deck duty for a further eight hours and then sleep. There was always a price to pay. No such thing as a free meal.

Overall, professional training as a BP officer was top priority from day one. During sea passages, a young cadet was expected to keep the ship's wheelhouse clean and tidy, escort pilots to and from the bridge during port transits and help with operational routines. Over time, a cadet would be introduced to the serious work of navigating ships. As confidence grew, the cadet would be taught the skill of coastal chart work, be encouraged to plot positions and to use radar plotting techniques. Understanding the legal 'Rule of the Road' anti-collision regulations 'word perfect' – was also an essential task facing any deck officer in training. BP had in place a daily study routine, and a regular exam scheme built into daily life at sea. Such study and a regular exam routine at sea was never abandoned in my experience. Excellence was encouraged. I was mentored by some first-rate officers, and I look back on my sea time as a BP officer cadet with great affection. I acquired a vast array of technical knowledge and quickly learned to apply it with growing confidence. My schoolboy days were well over.

I was alone on the surface of the oceans of the world. But never totally alone. Before going to sea, I began to read a Head Prefect prize from school: *The New English Bible*; and the clear Christian message of redemption finally changed me. So, in late 1962, I embraced a real awakening as a school leaver. Along with my overall success at the top end of senior school, I had become a self-serving, profane 1960s youth. However, in 1963, I proceeded to sea as a self-confessed Christian. This followed a time of soul searching, life changing faith and announcing to my surprised friends and family that I had found, in the words of slave trader John Newton: 'Amazing Grace… I once was blind, but now I see'. My mother decided I had somehow lost the plot; my stepfather declared, 'He will soon get over this faith business'. But this was much deeper than a church parade. My own evangelical awakening began slowly after reading the New Testament, hearing the Christ-centred message: 'For God so loved the world', (John 3:16), and noting an Anglican Bishop advocate daily prayer.

So, I was committed as I went off to sea; but rarely mocked at sea for my new-found faith. Thanks again to the grace of God and the kindness of strangers. A mature fellow Christian, a leading British army officer with 'theatre of war' experience, noted in 2021, that there are few atheists in a British bunker under fire. Likewise, there are few real atheists at sea. However, I quickly learned never to preach at my shipmates. It was better to walk the talk at sea. I was referred to as a 'Billy Graham' on one ship; but I took that as a compliment. Generally, I have always got on well with my fellow seafarers, including the hard drinking, hard living fellow-rovers we met from time to time. I also met many Christians from diverse cultures across the world.

Summary of my first East of Suez adventure voyage during 1963/4

During my life-changing job interview at BP Tanker HQ in the autumn term of 1962, it was suggested that I might voyage to Australia. This was an exciting prospect for a 16-year-old Midlands schoolboy. I had ventured across the Irish Sea in a ferry from Fishguard to Cork during the summer of 1961, travelling as a 15-year-old with five other senior scouts; plus, a similar mountain walking party the following summer in the Scottish Highlands. But Australia was something else. A taste of high-seas adventure was in the air. But first, join a ship aged 16.

I arrived with my sea-chest to a warm welcome aboard *British Cormorant* on 1st March 1963. I asked in my best seaman's voice, 'Where is she bound?' A gruff shipmate answered, 'Copenhagen'. It was a cold day at the BP Kent oil refinery on the Isle of Grain (Isle of Rain) as I began my career; it was to prove even colder in our voyaging area for the next three months: North Sea, the Baltic and the Norwegian Arctic. It was the end of one of the harshest European winters for decades. I had camped in winter mountains, but I had never experienced cold like the cold easterly wind in the North Sea, during a March gale blowing in from the Northern European Plain. It was raw. But I was having a great time. By way of contrast, I can still feel the warmth of a Copenhagen store as I walked ashore, and blustered my way through the language barrier, explaining my need for a warm winter hat. The Danish female assistant tried to explain that the navy-blue item in my hand was designed for a young woman. It was blue and warm, so I handed over my Danish Kroner and went back to my ship. It caused a few laughs amongst my shipmates, but I had a warm head. I also failed to impress the cheerful flaxen-haired Danish girl who sold me the hat. Limited social skills?

I soon discovered that my secondary mod education was no match to the social ease and confidence of fellow cadets from public schools who often pitched up at sea. It was clear that I had a lot to learn, as my first OIC, Captain Fred Cuffley, was quick to point out. But the Mate (First Officer) and the Second Mate (Navigator) kindly watched my back, generally looked after my interests and gave me lots of survival advice. I made myself useful, and quickly began to learn the basic rules of handling the post-WW2 British Merchant Navy. I could see that real challenges lay ahead. My family made the road journey to the Isle of Grain on one occasion and seemed very impressed by the whole atmosphere of *British Cormorant*. However, my mother's description of a BP Tanker as a luxury hotel was not quite accurate. But she seemed satisfied that I would survive. So, my 1963 journey began: Arctic seas to southern storms as a seaman now aged 17.

The sea-training I received as a Cadet Navigating Officer with BP, from day one, was some of the best training available to a young seaman serving in the UK Merchant Navy during those 1960s halcyon days. I would serve in four of BP's modern tankers: *British Cormorant, British Comet, British Signal* and *British Kestrel*. Then, in BP Tanker fashion, my last few weeks of sea-time as a cadet would be spent on the UK coast in a battered old vessel called *British Workman*. I can still smell the ancient accommodation and see the darkened alleyways of *British Workman* – or *British Workhouse* as she was known by serving crews.

Overall, we saw more than the sea. Copenhagen was just the start. Our 1963 cold-weather voyage routine continued for many weeks as we ventured into the Baltic ice, relieving the ice-bound Swedish Port of Malmo, as if all in a day's work. A local newspaper ran heroic winter grabbing headlines applauding the *British Cormorant* and her valiant crew: 'Oil Tanker Cuts through Ice'. Local buses can run. Hospitals are safe. We became heroes overnight. Following this, we ventured into the ice-free waters of the Norwegian Arctic Sea, with a cargo of aviation spirit for the NATO base located at Bodo, in Norway's Arctic Latitudes. Bodo was bitterly cold; but the sunshine tempted our Third Officer to spend an afternoon in swimming trunks on the deck above the navigation bridge (aptly called the Monkey Island). He got a tanning session under his belt, designed to impress his English girlfriend. I quickly came to view 1960s tanker officers as a hardy breed of men. I attempted to mimic their hardiness.

My weekly hand written training journal was signed off each week by the Captain: with technical details of life at sea and ports visited. My surviving journal covers my last two years of training, so I can only estimate the distances covered by the ship during my own 1963/64 voyages as a crew member in *British Cormorant*. Based on estimated sea-days, at an average speed of 15 knots, we covered over 85,000 nautical miles from Norway's Arctic seas to the Southern latitudes and back to the UK, with all stops along the way. Day and night; month after month of solid work. Our canny-Scot of a Chief Officer joined and left on the same day as me; I was a fresh-faced 'first-tripper'; he was married with three young children. Like me, he was almost 14 months away from home comfort. I got on well with 'Mr Mate' Tom Richardson; the only time we fell out was the day I used a can of off limits 'pay-off paint' on a routine job at sea. I can still hear his thunderous roar as he called me to give an account of myself. Our kindly Captain Pugh reminded me, in his own low-key debrief, that I should always clarify orders. BP Tanker training: I would eventually exchange a paint brush for a sextant. Three years later, serving in the identical *British Kestrel*, I would be appointed to the role of OOW as a 20-year-old. Training always pays dividends.

Back to my reflections as a 'first tripper'. After the cold spring of 1963 the *British Cormorant* ended her voyages in Scandinavian waters and entered the River Tyne for a dry-dock in South Shields. Brigham and Cowan's dry-dock was awash with shoreside activity as soon as the dock gates closed. The lower Tyne in 1963 was a mass of UK ships and seafarers. Sadly, those days are gone forever. As are small British tankers taking aviation spirit to Arctic NATO bases. In those halcyon days, the tanker SS *British Queen* was the pride of the BP fleet – 50,000 dwt of ocean-going splendour. Meanwhile, we sailed from the Tyne in the late spring of 1963, making a voyage to Tenerife before loading a high value cargo of lube oil. We sailed for southern seas via the Suez Canal. My first East of Suez adventure was just beginning as a 17-year-old Cadet Officer, still a tad wet behind the ears. Bound for Australia, New Zealand and the Southern Cross.

Memories from 1963: My voyage to Australia aged 17

Indian Ocean Midnight

East of Suez; our courses set for regions Antipodean.
Deck Watch changing at the midnight hour;
Faithful guardian night – sailing in company with
The presence of the silent zephyr breeze.
Reflected starlight on the ocean-face appears.
Our bioluminescent bow-wave – joins the wonders
Of the ink-black night. This gift of ancient stillness.
Above, the star-encrusted legends of eternity unfold;
Whispers of a guardian angel's wing? Behold
The transit of night-wandering constellations.
Untold depths of midnight silence – with
Unspoken questions into who we are?
Soft rain falling, like tears from northern homelands:
And at this lonely midnight hour, the steady beating
Of fragile, salt-stained, hearts of oak.
Wild rovers all: Seafaring Men.
Bound for South Australia and the Southern Cross.
Peter John Hill, 2020.

A first deep-sea voyage will leave its mark on any would-be professional seafarer. Overall, those first 14 months serving as a young Cadet Officer left a deep imprint, but no scars. I found my shipmates supportive and approachable. Religion and politics were both 'off the agenda' subjects amongst UK seafarers, but the motley

British Cormorant
in mid-ocean, 1963.

crew of the *British Cormorant* in 1963 welcomed my Christian ways in their midst, showing great toleration. All fond memories. I was being well cared for in my youthful circumstances; I can recall a bit of personal loneliness setting in during the long sea passage to Australia. Never homesick – but I was missing my pals in the UK. I would not admit it at the time, but at just 17, I think I missed my senior school sporting activity. However, any short-term blues were offset by being assigned to an Indian Ocean morning study and deck-work routine; plus, daily standing the midnight to 0400hrs Graveyard Watch as a crew member, for the whole voyage from the Red Sea to Western Australia. My ship and the Indian Ocean – plus good company on watch, and the magnitude of the whole cosmos. Bright new stars to remember night after night. I began to learn from the very professional approach of the Middle Watch OOW Second Mate, 'Bronco' Lane – in reality just a handful of years older than me; but with apparently endless knowledge of the sea, and maturity beyond his years. I developed a thirst for a similar level of knowledge, maturity and seamanship skill. It would take me a while to get there, even with the excellent mentoring and tuition provided by BP. But get there I would – by the age of 20.

I was walking taller by the time I arrived off the Aussie coast in those youthful years. We anchored south of Kwinana, our Western Australia arrival port. I had my own Cadet Cabin on the Captain's Deck on the ship's starboard side. I recall looking out through salted glass to see a low profile of a distant Australian shore. I was amazed that a few months after leaving school, I was at the beginning of a Southern Hemisphere voyage of discovery. We arrived at our Western Australia refinery destination and made the ship secure. Aussie soil. My older shipmates advised me to take a horse to Fremantle. They described it as a cowboy town. It was wet. Just like the UK – but with warm, steady rain. A real sub-tropical feel.

I made a Sunday trip into Fremantle soon after arriving. I hitched a ride from the Roman Catholic ship-visitor. We had an engaging conversation on the road journey. But it was a one-way trip. When he dropped me off, he said I should pray for him. He would say a prayer for me. I needed someone to pray: I had no idea how I would get back to my very distant ship. But, in the exuberance of my youthful ways, I was not too concerned. I had the address of a Fremantle Aussie Gospel church. And I arrived ready for a 6:30pm evening service – just like the UK? It was still raining. Real heavy downpours. 6:30pm Western Australian Time arrived – and then left in a soggy haze. Deserted streets meant all the cowboys had gone to their Aussie beds. Not a Sheila in sight. I was in solitary confinement until 8:00pm when a car turned up and doors of the evangelical church hall opened. A local family took me home for a very late supper. I was suddenly part of a Christian kinship group again. Afterwards, we covered the miles back to the Kwinana refinery gates in a Holden station wagon. I then walked the midnight miles back to my welcoming ship, through endless lines of pipes and tank farms. Welcome to Western Australia. Throughout almost 14 months serving in *British Cormorant*, my own bunk was always a welcome sight. My ship was my home.

The challenge of being young and at sea. A degree from the University of Life. The run ashore in rain-swept Fremantle set a pattern for many months ahead of me during my first 'East of Suez' adventure. I would hitch rides, walk or catch public transport in whatever Southern Hemisphere port my ship was visiting. Many runs ashore awaited me as a young seaman. But trouble never found me in any seaport; and I never went searching for trouble. I have since heard first-hand stories of seamen handing over their wallets at knifepoint after passing through the dock gates. I learned to walk very tall ashore, without a moment of anxiety, even in South Africa and India. Great memories to carry through life.

We sailed from the Kwinana refinery, and ahead of us was more of upbeat Australia and New Zealand; plus, months of sea-time before returning to the UK. The sea-state in the Southern Hemisphere was also very upbeat. Once south of Fremantle we cleared Cape Leeuwin and began to shape a course to the east; we were soon in the orbit of the Great Australian Bight. The sea was awesome. I was 17 years old, and a very long way from my home port. We were a ship full of wild-rovers, surrounded by the dangers of the ocean and the many snares surrounding sailors ashore. In those wild waters, the sea washed over our fore deck day after day. And there were real hazards ashore.

In those first few months I had witnessed many new things: North Sea ice; Arctic waters; bitter cold; a Suez Canal transit; the Red Sea; the vast calm of the Indian Ocean; the splendour of the Cosmos. Most things were awe-inspiring. But I also began to witness the dark side of the human condition. Not everything I witnessed at sea was uplifting. Many times, I observed my fellow seamen returning from their own shoreside pleasures, often in a very sorry state, always at midnight or later; and always totally legless after heavy drinking ashore. That master of seafaring tales, Joseph Conrad, spoke of the grand illusions of life dispensed in glasses, sold to the crew members of southern-going ships. The *British Cormorant* was the same as any ship at sea in the 1960s. I learned never to be naive towards the many hazards awaiting far-from-home sailors. The survival techniques I learned on my first voyage 'East of Suez' would remain with me for life. It began with – always give smiling strangers a very wide berth. It was a valuable lesson.

We were to see plenty of strangers during our sojourn in and around the Indian Ocean. On one mega voyage we left Kwinana for Durban, then sailed north east to Bombay and then back to Western Australia. However, overall, we would spend some time on the Australian coast, including Sydney, Adelaide and Melbourne and back to Kwinana (Fremantle) Western Australia – before sailing for the New Zealand ports of Wellington, Auckland and Whangārei. Our various voyage cargoes consisted of 'parcels' of lube oil, which often gave us cheerful discharge jetties close to centres of population; and very slow discharge rates of cargo from ship to shore would always provide us with longer than normal periods alongside. Once again, we had every opportunity to enjoy a run ashore and explore. On occasions officers and cadets would launch lifeboats to run engines; at times I would swim from the moored lifeboat; but I was aware of the shark warnings on Aussie beaches (and we had the luxury of a shark-free ship's plunge pool).

We touched the beating heart of Australia and New Zealand in 1963; and its mainly urban populations generally made us all very welcome. South Australia, Victoria and New South Wales were a breath of fresh air after the remoteness of Western Australia. I was once looked after by a ship-visiting Christian family in Adelaide and, just before sailing, gained crew 'brownie points' when the father and daughter delivered me back to the ship in the luxury of an immaculate vintage limo. I was also greeted on a Sunday morning by a ship-visiting ex-seaman in New Zealand by the name of Doug Turner. I had worked through the night, but Doug took me home to his wife and family for the whole of Sunday. I was made very welcome. These Christian families had a telephone network and I would often be greeted at short notice in the next port of call. Home from home in a faraway place. Over the years at sea, I would see this pattern of genuine Christian hospitality repeated all over the world. The grace of God; the kindness of trustworthy strangers. There is a paradox here: we all have to learn the survival skills which indicate those who cannot be trusted. I quickly learned never to take anyone at face value. I never made a mistake.

Tragic news was received onboard during a routine day in an Australian port of call: on 22nd November 1963, US President JFK was assassinated – shot by a sniper in Dallas whilst travelling in an open car. This was grim news indeed in the swinging 60s, whatever hemisphere you were in. Kennedy was an icon of youthful hope in an upbeat decade. LBJ was now at the helm of the Western World. Suddenly, news from the real world of political drama came to a British ship and crew on the far side of the planet. The mood onboard *British Cormorant* remained sombre for days. Under the bright skies of an Australian spring, bad news travelled fast: Kennedy was dead. It was time to think of home.

By Christmas 1963, most crew members serving in *British Cormorant* were ready to be homeward bound as we sailed away from New Zealand for the final time. One further call into Bombay on our passage homewards towards Suez – and we were almost there. Plans of mice and men. It was now 1964: BP had one final New Year surprise for a restless crew. An exhausted crew. With Bombay as our new 'homeport' – we were to spend a further two months on the coast of the Indian sub-continent. The jewel in our crown: regular voyages between Bombay and Budge-Budge. Not everyone has heard of Budge-Budge. As I write, I can find it via Google, located south of Calcutta on the silt-shifting Hooghly River (Kata Ganga) and approached via the Bay of Bengal. A remote 1964 tanker jetty if ever there was one. According to the photographic evidence, Budge-Budge is much developed since our visit in 1964. But, etched in my memory, I can still see the small dhows drifting on the stream, carrying a whole haystack as cargo; and birds sitting on bloated human remains as they too drifted past. Like the wandering albatross of the southern seas, 1960s India left a deep impression on a young seaman. However, there were uplifting times as I walked ashore in Bombay. I was made welcome by a family who managed a city-centre printing company producing books and pamphlets. I would walk through the crowded city streets to their business premises and be taken home for meals. But I was starting to experience cabin fever and was ready for our return to the UK pay-off port after almost a year's service in the ship. However, I received some welcome support and encouragement from the Thompson and Durham families in Bombay, plus warm hospitality and friendship from Indian nationals. I was still a youth of 17.

Eventually our Bombay to Budge-Budge voyages ended; we were homeward bound. My sea-chest was packed by the time we cleared Port Said. After almost 14 months, I was ready for my first spell of long shore leave. I would enjoy the luxury of 10 weeks at home before returning to the sea and officer training.

There would be many more voyages as a Cadet Officer during my years of sea-training. Thirty-six months of 'sea time' was required, with periods of leave between serving in each of four BP Tankers in my case. (My mid sea-training course at South Shields Marine and Technical College counted as 'sea-time'). Following my first long leave, I joined *British Comet*, an Italian built crude oil 'super tanker' of its day. The voyage pattern was to be very different from the Euro/Scandinavian, Australian/New Zealand and Indian coastal work enjoyed during service in *British Cormorant*. Our 1964 primary role in *British Comet* was to load cargoes of crude oil in distant Lake Maracaibo, Venezuela or in the northern Gulf oil ports – usually Abadan, located South East of Basra. Our main discharge terminals were generally in the busy European North Sea coastal refineries such as the facility located near the German Port of Wilhelmshaven. We spent long months voyaging between one blisteringly hot location to cold northern European terminals. Once loaded, we were required to proceed LEFO

(Land's End For Orders). It was generally a disciplined but mundane way of life, with much professional study time, plus notable shipboard days of mirth or chaos. I will deal first with nautical mirth in an account of a woman in white.

In any act of comedy there is always a victim, at sea or ashore. This account has a leading female victim in the person of the wife of our tanker Captain. The immaculate white tropical uniform of the ship's Master was worn in the tropics, even when hammering me at table-tennis during our frequent matches after lunch. The Captain was a well-turned-out nautical soul, very proud of his station in life. His wife was the same; she reminded me of our own late Queen. One afternoon, with the ship anchored in the eastern Mediterranean, she requested that we sail around the ship in a lifeboat under full canvas. The fact that there was not a breath of wind made it an interesting prospect: a cruise in the sun. Nevertheless, Number One starboard lifeboat was launched; and a very smart Captain and his wife joined us as we lowered away in the style portrayed in the *Titanic* movies. The white clad couple were looked after by two deck officers and four cadets. The Captain and his wife were in safe hands. Nothing could go wrong to cause a stain on a white tropical uniform or the matching white dress of his dignified wife. We were all tempting nautical fate. The saying is well known, 'Worse things happen at sea'. It would be a noteworthy lifeboat cruise.

The weather did not change, so we drifted for an hour in the warm sunshine until afternoon 'smoko' when a brew-up beckoned. We decided it was time for silver-service. The Captain's wife sat upright on the thwarts like a monarch, eager to step from her launch to the cheers of onlookers. We jolly sailors secured the falls (lifting tackle) to be raised in splendour to the embarkation gate. All routine. However, a waste discharge pipe was positioned right in line with the lifeboat as it rose from the sea. More accurately, the discharge was right in line with the head of the Captain's wife. A very poor ship design feature. In the 1960s, most ships' waste water was untreated and went directly into the sea. The Captain's wife took home vivid memories of the day. It might have been her honeymoon cruise when she was also crowned. To her credit she did not flinch. A dignified exit from the lifeboat into a hot shower. Rather you than me ma'am.

The next notable *British Comet* 1964 incident happened in the discharge Port of Antwerp. During our return from the Gulf via the Suez Canal, the deck crew had been deployed on a mission to repaint the Italian built tanker. The task had been well executed by the day-workers, led by competent Able Seamen and the Boatswain (Bosun). The vessel arrived in Antwerp looking like a royal yacht. Her grey decks had been the subject of hours of toil with chipping hammers and paint rollers. We arrived in Antwerp and discharged our cargo of Gulf crude oil, all without incident. Before sailing from the berth for another voyage to the tropics, the ship was required to load seawater ballast into various tanks, all containing a residue of our crude oil cargo. That was the situation I walked into as an 18-year-old cadet, when I joined the Second Officer at midnight to oversee a routine dock-water ballasting operation, prior to sailing at daylight.

All was quiet as the midnight hour passed. The deck crew were ashore tasting the nightlife of the port; the Captain and Chief Officer were sleeping before the daylight departure; ballast was being pumped into various empty cargo tanks. It was my job to monitor the flow of ballast into three athwartship tanks on the foredeck. But I misjudged the high rate of flow into these tanks. As the Second Officer and I discussed an issue of ship stability in the ship's office, the alarm was raised by a duty Pumpman: we had struck oil on the foredeck. Ballast inflow had overflowed: tonnes of residue crude oil floating on water had shot through an ullage pipe onto the freshly painted decks. The spillage was prevented from entering the dock by the routine blocking of the deck level scuppers; but the crude oil sludge had covered all the newly painted decks. At this dramatic moment, our sailors were stumbling from shoreside to their bunks, therefore, all hands were required on deck at 0100hrs to clean up the entire mess. The task would take the whole of the remaining night hours. The new paintwork was in a sad state. Afterwards came the enquiry; but no voice of blame was ever heard. The whole episode and train-smash incident was quickly forgotten. Nobody shot a word of anger in my direction. After a few days, I went to see the Chief Officer with apologies for any neglect on my part whilst on duty. This simple act somehow appeared to go in my favour, and the issue of an overflow in Antwerp was closed. No attempt at a cover-up. Accidents will happen: human error.

I was well into my second year as a seafarer, spending my second Christmas at sea, before leaving *British Comet* on 26th January 1965. After a short period of leave, I joined her Italian built sister *British Signal* on 6th March 1965, after a North Sea ferry crossing with other officers to the Hook of Holland. We joined the ship in Antwerp. I entered the senior phase of my deck officer training, and was beginning to find my feet as a seaman. I would learn new skills during my deployment serving in *British Signal*; and during a planned dry-docking on the Tyne, I would rub shoulders again with 'Geordie-land' – an area where my future wife was growing up. A new dawn was breaking. I was making intellectual, professional and personal progress and was still just 18 years old as I joined the Italian built ship – my third BP Tanker. My 19th birthday quickly passed at sea. The general pattern of life of *British Signal* was similar to *British Comet*: crude oil cargo; regular signals to the ship after loading: 'Land's End for Orders'. But a different pattern of ports prevailed including Antwerp, Bougie (Algeria) and the Gulf Port of Mena al Ahmadi, plus other Gulf oil terminals.

My navigational skill-set would be dominated by a clear grasp of position fixing at sea using mid-morning and noon sextant observations of the Sun's altitude. This kind of position fixing was the marine navigator's trade mark, before the postmodern era arrived with the advent of the computer age. Fixing by satellite was a far-off innovation: in the 1960s and 70s all deep-sea deck officers carried their own marine sextants as part of the job, and computed long-hand with the aid of Norrie's Tables. As a raw cadet, I learned spherical trigonometry and celestial navigation from first principles. From my new training berth as a Senior Cadet, life at sea was becoming a rewarding academic and practical challenge. Once again, I was encouraged at sea by a corps of highly skilled BP deck officers.

It is worthwhile setting out the noble art and skill of fixing a ship's position at sea by sextant altitude of heavenly bodies. The maths involved is in reality not so advanced; more of a niche learning curve. There are many expertly written books which unpack celestial navigation including D.A. Moore's, *Basic Principles of Marine Navigation*: Stanford Maritime. In practical terms, I adopted the well-known Marcq St Hilaire methodology, also known as the *Intercept Method*.

An *Intercept* is the difference between the *observed Zenith Distance (ZX)* of a spherical *PZX triangle* (from sextant altitude obs) and the *calculated ZX* – as derived from your Estimated Position (EP). An accurate EP is the all-important starting point for the *Intercept*, with your Position Line (PL) running at 90° to the end of the *Intercept*. Add the haversine formula and you have cracked it!!

Spherical trigonometry is an enjoyable subject central to calculations, with trig ratios, (cosine and haversine), and PZX spherical triangles being the key critical navigational concepts. The basic skill is to transfer a Position Line (PL) to your Admiralty chart (your Position Line always runs at 90° to the *azimuth/bearing* of the observed body). By taking two or more observations, either moments apart or at a recorded time/distance interval, the marine navigator can 'work up' a ship's position represented by the intersection of transferred Position Lines: i.e. a simple cross on the chart. Also, taking a Meridian (Noon) observation of the Sun or a twilight observation of the Pole Star, (visible in the Northern Hemisphere and always bearing north), results in producing the mariner's latitude (i.e. an east-west Position Line on the chart). Critically, Position Lines at sea require accurate sextant observations, plus accurate time keeping and the application of the haversine formula. Accurate working is part of the navigator's skill: all on the plane of the observer's Rational Horizon. It takes time to learn these skills; but clear textbooks and good tutors always help motivated students.

Summary: Textbook clarification of these issues can be found under 'Position Lines' in all books published on the subject of celestial navigation, available from nautical publishers. This will be of interest to RYA students as well as to student mariners. (The 'Longitude by Chronometer' method is also of interest).

As a 16-year-old schoolboy, the author took two attempts to pass GCE maths; and it took two further years of study to get to grips with the basic Principles of Marine Navigation. And there was much more to come. I left *British Signal* to spend three months of focused study at South Shields Marine and Technical College in September 1965, under the key direction of Captain D.M. 'Robbie' Robinson. As stated earlier, the South Shields course of nautical science subjects would establish my adult academic approach for years to come. Twenty years later, with Captain Robinson as Head of Marine School at South Shields, his reference would secure my place on a full-time degree programme, which would open employment doors for the rest of my working life, and also lead directly to 25 years of regular sail training experience to the age of 69 years.

As indicated, South Shields Dept of Nautical Science was a place of intensity in autumn 1965: wall to wall study for twelve weeks, balanced by several outside visits to shipyards, dry-docks, Coast Radio Stations and Air-Sea Rescue units plus one night a week in the college gym, led by a PTI. Probably the most stimulating full term of learning anywhere in my own experience before or since. There were 27 cadet officers on my course. I finished the course in 3rd place, and managed to lead the field in the examination paper set for Principles of Navigation (87%). I then joined *British Kestrel* in January 1966 full of knowledge and confidence. I was destined to leave the ship in July after European coastal voyages and a further voyage to the Indian Coast. The entire period of service in *British Kestrel* brought about many new challenges: our Captain died suddenly on a voyage from Port Said to the UK; we took his body to Gibraltar for repatriation by air. His replacement was a jolly seaman: Captain Freeman, who immediately appointed me as OOW. I took over sole responsibility for the safe 8-12 navigational watchkeeping – morning and evening for the last two months of my sea time as a 20-year-old cadet. I then returned to South Shields Marine and Technical College to gain my qualification as 2nd Mate. I passed all parts of the exam at my first attempt and qualified before my 21st birthday.

Overall, my passage from youth to manhood was crowned by the whole BP experience, two productive terms at nautical college, plus my first life-changing professional qualification; and always the memory of an albatross battling the southern seas. The grace of God and the kindness of strangers saw me through. Overall, the sea bestowed my lifetime work ethic. Tall ships were on my radar.

Wandering Albatross: Acrylic sketch by the author, 2015.

The author on shore-leave in Bombay during OOW service in the BP Tanker British Kestrel (1966). I would officially qualify as a deck officer in January 1967.

Chapter 7

The Arrow of Time – Fear no more the lightning flash

By the age of 20, I had progressed from schoolboy to an experienced seafarer, with early service as Officer of the Watch in *British Kestrel* deployed East of Suez. I was hardly out of my teenage years. Trust is a powerful lever in life experience. A high level of self-confidence is inspired by being a trusted team player. I did not realise at the time, but the trust that placed me as the solo OOW on the bridge of a modern BP tanker night and day, was to prove invaluable. I can remember my first helm order to avoid fishing vessels in the Bay of Biscay; and the first time I called the Captain to report an unusual marine hazard. My entire experience at sea as a cadet officer moulded both my work ethic and academic approach for the rest of my working life. Early seafaring fulfilled a real need in my youth for demanding situations to be faced with confidence. There is no doubt at all that the sea provided my own pathway to early maturity; we must all be prepared to learn survival skills within a unit of focused team players, such as fellow seafarers. However, there is a heavy cost attached to spending months away from the trivial round – confined in the close quarters of a ship at sea.

As an athlete in my youth, I had tried various regimes at sea to remain fit, agile and strong. I observed the effect of long months spent at sea: hale and hearty fellow sea-rovers could become very unfit. The most alarming effect was noticed when I observed a senior ship's officer in middle age, return from a simple trip ashore. He made his way on board and then spent 20 minutes recovering from the effort. I had never observed this competent officer with a cigarette in his hands; but his lungs could not cope with the effort of simple long-term walking and then climbing a gangway to gain entry. Lack of exercise carries a high cost.

In addition to the fitness issue, I also observed the long periods away from home in the 1960s, and the very little time spent by seafarers with growing children. I seriously intended, at some point, to marry and also raise a family. All these considerations probably fed my subconscious and my decision to reject BP's offer of a contract as Third Officer in early 1967. Clear 20/20 hindsight is a wonderful thing. As a ship's officer, I had learned to make firm decisions; but I lacked in my youth the key life experience to know that BP was offering me a pathway to senior status, plus financial security in early life. Therefore, as a direct result of my shallow youthful choice, I would eventually face several real financial issues in my early 20s, as I attempted to establish a secure life ashore. I should have recognised a generous life opportunity when it presented itself on a golden BP plate. Nevertheless, ashore, I was about to gain real hard-nosed experience which would eventually lead me back to seafaring. The challenge of my chosen journey as I launched into my 20s unfolds below. (I would at least be at home to support the arrival of three healthy children – all born while I was still in my 20s; and all breech deliveries: I was told to leave the delivery suite).

After enjoying the early freedom of the seven seas and early exam success as a navigating officer, in 1967 I returned to live for a while with my mother and stepfather. Relations were generally good: we were all adults together. I had no real problem finding work ashore, and was engaged first in a civil engineering project constructing a complex National Grid site in Feckenham, Worcestershire – for the Central Electricity Generating Board (CEGB). After some basic on-site training, I was placed in charge of collecting and crush-testing samples of high-quality concrete used in base construction across the massive site: a role for a student of civil engineering in all honesty. However, I became a valued team player. I was out in all weathers; and in time moved on to further technical responsibilities: site levelling and general theodolite work. All sound experience day after day, working with an odd mixture of rough-and-ready labourers and very experienced civil engineers. Banter and good pay prevailed.

However, I had other things in mind and decided I wanted to work in a people focused service with statutory responsibilities. This was a mirror of my recent seafaring. I should have applied to the police or fire service. I had fitness, life experience and proven people skills to offer. (Or teaching – but that meant training school and no income). With many choices, I eventually walked into a City of Birmingham Corporation office, and declared my interest in working for them. Three months later, I was called to interview and appointed to a trainee job on a basic starting salary and vehicle allowance. I quickly learned to drive; and I passed my driving test at the first attempt, after taking six lessons from an instructor. I was then, after very little formal training, (but with youthful gravitas on my side), given a caseload and promoted to the role which appears on our 1968 Marriage Certificate – Mental Welfare Officer (MWO). This was to be a low paid, eye-opening task. It involved being awarded 'warranted authority' to fulfil Local Authority duties under prevailing Mental Health Law: exercising detention to psychiatric hospitals, of mentally ill persons resident within the Birmingham city limits and 'sectioned' under Act of Parliament. This included any emergency psychiatric admissions. 'Sectioned' against the individuals will was the key operational concept. This involved being on call day or night, depending on the duty roster.

During the night hours in long-gone 1968, the solo 'MWO on call' covered the whole City of Birmingham. Typically, I would receive a phone call from Ambulance Control at 2:00am to deploy, in the night hours, to some part of the city, and, with police back-up on hand, administer a 'section' and then supervise admission to a secure local NHS psychiatric unit. All very demanding and life enhancing aged 22. I took pride in the fact that every compulsory 'section' done under my supervision was without injury to any party. But, as a recently married man, with a child on the way, the salary was poor; so, given a reality check, I was compelled by circumstances to move on. I could have avoided all the stress and strain by taking BP's early seafaring offer. Live and learn. But no experience is ever wasted in my view, providing you gain some wisdom from the choice involved. I smile as I write and look back as my wife and I faced the challenge of building a future together in 1968. Some of my early choices were imperfect.

More life experience, and its normal ups and downs, was waiting in the wings. Having established a reputation for flexibility, I quickly moved on from my 1968 Mental Welfare Officer duties in Birmingham – to managing a team of hard-bitten roof tilers working for a national contractor in the North East of England.

My Bride: Elaine Hill nee Overman, Wedding Day July 1968.

Something of a contrast. The roof tiling outfit was keen to employ former seafaring officers or former police officers. It was the late 1960s – and roof tiling was all about sober men managing hard drinking men at work. This commercial move was to give me an immediate boost in fortune – better salary, company cars and bonus payments meant that my new responsibilities, as a husband and father, were managed without a problem. We began to prosper. A year after our 1968 wedding, our first child had safely arrived: Brian Peter Hill. (Brian would become the police officer to mirror the Warner side of my family, who had produced a superintendent in the former Worcestershire Constabulary).

The management of roof tilers in County Durham would quickly lead to overall income stability, which meant that throughout life we did not look back. Despite normal life setbacks, we would never suffer real financial hardship. In 1972, we purchased two spacious flats, one above the other, in a Tyneside town; then, after a major refurbishment project, we occupied the top flat and rented out the lower flat to elderly sisters. Family life was here to stay. But there is always a price to pay for any honest progress in life. The price involved in my roofing contracts combined long hours of site supervision and attention to costing details. Tendering took time and effort; and I managed to secure some very demanding contracts, including the large-scale removal and re-tiling of domestic roofs (whilst residents remained in their homes).

Materials were always in plentiful supply; and I always worked until after midnight on Friday evenings, managing paperwork for the following week on site. I also spent many hours trying to balance my mobile workforce of up to twelve experienced men against the constant pressure from site agents to keep to their own house production targets. Lighter moments surfaced: during a routine in-house company training course, delegates were each given a copy of the Chairman's book – tracing the page-turning history of the concrete roof tile. Essential bedtime reading without doubt. In reality, there was little time for such reading pleasures. Roof tiling was demanding work for all concerned; but it led me to ever greater commercial opportunities and growing financial rewards to provide for a family.

After two years, and the birth of Brent, another promising offer was made in the field of solving material handling and storage problems. This suited the site-surveyor in me – and I moved on to spend many hours surveying warehouse sites. I had a drawing board at home, produced quotations and presented my solutions to storage and material handling problems at boardroom level across County Durham. I worked to ever-increasing monthly targets under an area manager; eventually, I was promoted to a senior role, with responsibility for area technical sales staff. Once again, we prospered financially; and in 1974, I landed a role as

Brian: Eldest child, born 27th June 1969. WM Police.

Brent: Middle child. Road Traffic law/ WM Police.

Janette: Youngest child: aged 1 as I returned to sea. Successful Graphic Designer/Book Illustrator/Artist.

Area Manager for a fork lift truck rental company. My patch, this time, was the whole North of England above Yorkshire. By this time, my earnings were really growing; the arrival of our daughter Janette and a luxury company car completed the success story. But I had not considered the effect of debilitating stress. Life changing events lay ahead as I burned the midnight oil.

Commercial life in the UK during the 1970s was far from easy. We suffered all manner of strikes in key industries; we suffered power cuts; oil prices went through the roof; inflation took over. It was difficult for any company to control costs. My own North East business took a hit. My fleet of fork lift trucks was being battered in the docklands, foundries and heavy industry of the North Country. My rentals prospered; but my maintenance costs were sky-high and out of control. One day it all hit me like an express train. I began to shake without reason and lost the ability to concentrate; plus, pains in my chest for no clinical reason. I thought that my end game was near. My doctor said it was simply stress. I was eventually advised by my GP to give it all up. There was only one solution which would provide immediate change and preserve my income. I would go back to seafaring.

I made the decision in early 1976 to join Manchester Liners. It would prove to be a life-enhancing decision. With three young children, and our daughter hardly a year old, I found myself leaving home in a taxi in the early morning rain: and that drive into the unknown was the hardest thing I had ever done. With my wife and children beginning another normal day without me, my train pulled out of Newcastle Central Station. I had a battered suitcase containing my uniform; I had a small wooden box containing my second-hand marine sextant; I had a lump in my throat as big as a golf ball. One of my all-time low points indeed; again, in a place where life could only improve. We all face hard choices at times. I was 29 years old; I would now be faced with rekindling a sea career. However, the grace of God and the real kindness of strangers remained a living reality. And somewhere in the distant southern seas, a lone albatross was riding out a storm. A silver lining to every cloud in my sky.

I joined Manchester Liners for a fresh start at sea. I was greatly encouraged when I was told I would work a six week on/three week off routine. In addition, my shaking was gone; and so was the pain in my chest. Always, there is a price to pay in life. But light was beginning to dawn on a new day. The North Atlantic Ocean would be my companion for the next two years. Time to heal. Time to settle my mind. And my family was secure in our comfortable Tyneside home.

Chapter 8

Manchester Liners – The wind like a whetted knife

In my late 20s, with my newly refurbished property project complete, young wife, three smiling young children plus a mortgage, I signed up for deck officer service in the newly established North Atlantic sea-container shipping routes: Manchester to Montreal. It was to be as demanding as my youth voyages with BP, but away from warm climates and into wild seas, grey skies and ice. The following sea-verse, written in later life, sums up much of my seafaring between 1976 and 1978. Service with Manchester Liners would leave a unique deep imprint.

Brothers of the Western Ocean
Lamp of the morning rising over the sea
The light of Venus gone
Parallel wake stretching
To the eastern horizon;
And then 'The Crowd' appears.
Salt-stained mixture
Of madness and mirth
Raw texture of humanity.
Welded as they are by mercantile fraternity;
Windswept survivors: their seafaring voyages defined
By frozen mornings; St Lawrence River pilotage; Montreal.
Storm-bound in mid Atlantic; mountainous seas; furious line-squall;
Yet they survive harsh driving snow and rain;
Come summer Belle Isle 'bergs;
Come brutal hurricane; come loneliness with all its pain.
Our bosun with his iron grip. Beer-belly; faded jeans.
Ship's carpenter: Happy Jack – at sea too long. It seems
He carries in his head, the knack of getting nowhere fast.
Has a picture of his woman in Rio. Wishful dreams?
Mersey bound. More days; more dollars; then home at last.
Peter John Hill, 1997.

Heavy weather in Tall Ship: Author's painting.

Becalmed in Tall Ships' Race: Author's photograph. Atlantic voyages 1976–77 were good preparation for changing weather conditions experienced under sail to 2015.

Manchester Liners was an established shipping company with a proud history of brave seaman and strong ships, well documented by Nick Robins in his book *Manchester Liners – An Extraordinary Story*, Bernard McCall, 2011. Robins' book is a mine of information on company ships from the ill-fated *Manchester Enterprise* (ML service 1898–99) which he reports as foundered in 1899 on passage from Liverpool to Montreal. The record is followed by a reference to *Manchester Trader* (ML service 1898–1912); and, under different owners, sunk in a torpedo attack on passage from Cardiff to Spezia in 1916. In similar circumstances, the *Manchester Commerce* (ML service 1899–1914) was sunk by a mine on passage from Manchester to Montreal. The list of Manchester Liners, including war casualties by mine and gunfire, moves on in researched detail until the advent of WW2, when the grim war list of shipping loss continues… *Manchester Hero* (ML service 1916–1937) sunk by torpedo in 1941, under different owners, on passage from Naples to Tripoli; *Manchester Brigade* (ML service 1918–1940) sunk by torpedo on passage from Manchester to Montreal. The ML list continues until Robins' final war-loss entry: *Manchester Citizen* (ML service 1925–1943) sunk by torpedo on passage from Freetown to Lagos. A vivid picture of shipping loss is brought to mind – not as a result of iceberg or hurricane, but gunfire and torpedo attack. The 2020 UK Annual Festival of Remembrance reported 30,000 British Merchant Seamen lost to enemy action in two world wars. Manchester Liners took an enormous toll. Brave hearts indeed. UK merchant seamen – vital in any UK war effort.

Manchester Liners survived years of ocean crossings and conflict since its creation by Sir Christopher Furness in 1898, as detailed in Nick Robins' account.

In its earlier days, it offered a service dictated by Northern Hemisphere seasons between Manchester and Montreal (to St John, New Brunswick when the mighty St Lawrence was frozen over). When the late 20th Century was faced with the incremental growth and standardisation of the shipping containers by sea, rail and road, Manchester Liners elected to order specialised ships to provide the mercantile service across the North Atlantic. This innovation influenced my life.

In his book, Nick Robins concludes his brief overview,

> *The link with the City of Manchester underlines the important role that both Manchester Liners and the Manchester Ship Canal Company had in wealth creation in the North West of England during the 20th Century. Robins quotes Sir Frederick West: Of the many things our city (Manchester) has done to inspire a proper sense of pride in its citizens, nothing stirs the mind so much as the cutting of the Manchester Ship Canal, which turned, as with a magic wand, Manchester, an inland city, into a great port.*

This North West England inland port was established in 1894 when the ship canal was officially opened. The first of many cargo-services by sea was then established between Manchester and Belfast. An economic breakthrough.

In 1976, I joined *Manchester Concorde* as a company deck officer. I was made to feel welcome from day one. My skills from my BP sea-training came flooding home. It was good to be back at sea, albeit facing a different set of nautical challenges, including whatever the North Atlantic weather elected to brew up. Such weather could prove to be wild and uncomfortable whatever the season of the year. Furthermore, the job came with a guarantee – Canadian winters were bitterly cold. Beware. Again, I joined not knowing what I had let myself in for, and would stay in the North Atlantic service for two memorable years.

Our Western Ocean voyage patterns followed Great Circle routes depending on the season, (and ice reports), and the expected Atlantic weather systems. Broadly speaking, once clear of the Mersey it was either northern or southerly courses to clear the Irish Sea. Duty captains also opted for different weather routes, and went by nicknames such as Hurricane Askew and Fairweather Phil, which indicated the preference of the individual ship master. But either way, they were seamen, and extreme weather was always avoided in a seamanlike manner. Safety of containers on deck was paramount, along with general ship safety. The North Channel route might also include a brief visit to Clydeside and the Port of Greenock. It always rains in Greenock. Good preparation for grey Atlantic skies.

Once clear of coastal shipping and the shelter of the Irish Sea it was the 'best-speed sea route' to the north of Newfoundland and Belle Isle Strait during the summer season, or southern Newfoundland and Cape Race in the coldest season. Ice could always become a menace – summer icebergs coming into the Atlantic from the Davis Strait during the warmer seasons, and winter pack ice in the Gulf of the St Lawrence. The four North Atlantic container ships under the Manchester Liners House Flag were built for the ice conditions. Other less robust merchant ships had a history of being caught in the Gulf of St Lawrence winter pack. Dangers included crushing by ice pressure. My personal notes from 1976 indicate many hazards. Since the 1987 loss of the ferry *Herald of Free Enterprise*, UK authorities have taken a much closer interest in Safety of Life at Sea (SOLAS).

Personal reflections: Manchester – Montreal deck officer voyage notes.

The year was 1976. Every week from Manchester, a red hulled ship, one of four Manchester Liners, sailed from the heart of the inland Salford Quays with a cargo of red boxes. The destination: Montreal, Province of Québec, Canada. Winter or summer the seafaring routine continued, come fair wind or foul. The red ships were deep-sea container vessels; the red boxes the secure containers – all part of a 20th Century revolution in the transport of cargo around the globe. If you produced medical equipment in Stockport for a surgery in Saskatoon, this was the route to take. By land and stormy sea; door to door; service with a nautical smile. Your equipment arrived by road at the 1976 container terminal in a 20-foot-long red container: from the lorry to the dock; from the dock to the ship; from the ship to the Montreal terminal; then, by highway or Canadian Pacific rail-road to customers' geographical locations in Saskatoon or beyond.

After several days loading our outward-bound cargo of containers, (faster cargo turnaround in the high-tech 21st Century), the red ship was made ready for the canal transit, Mersey pilotage and the open sea. Two hours before the container ship was due to sail, officers and crew took over from the loading team. The sailing crew completed all pre-departure checks including navigation preps and engines. All non-sailing personnel and visitors proceeded ashore. The ship started to breathe, as two pilots joined the team in the combined wheelhouse and chartroom. Marine engineers were on stand-by. Deck teams mustered at mooring stations fore and aft. The order was given to let-go; the ship's mass of steel and technology was pulled clear of the berth by tugs; slowly swinging her in the cold water of the canal basin; and the ship's head was then made steady. The red ship made its slow way towards the Mersey. (Within 30 hours she would be pitching into the swells of the Atlantic as she left the Irish coast on her westward course). As she cleared the first canal lock, local well-wishers left their cars to wave at us; young girls blew their kisses to our 1970s all-male crew. An outward-bound ship was cause for good cheer and celebration as evening began to close in. Navigation lights burned. From the shore, all looked warm and comfortable onboard. The experienced sailors knew what to expect as we all settled down to the task; the 24/7 routine of seafarers' iron sea-duty kicked in.

The ship canal gave little pleasure to the senses. On summer days it was bleak; on short winter days it was cold and grey. The pace was slow as the ship made her way towards Liverpool and the Mersey, with canal company tugs made fast at the bow and the stern. Our two pilots remained on duty in the wheelhouse – one as helmsman, the second having the 'con' (giving the helm and telegraph orders). Our Captain was on call, but generally left the ship in the hands of the pilots and the duty OOW. Things could go wrong at short notice. Ships were known to go aground during a canal transit, or even knock down the heavy gates of a lock. However, normally a transit was uneventful and Eastham Lock was reached 10 hours after leaving Manchester. At Eastham, the ship entered the Mersey. With darkness closing in and the open sea beckoning, Manchester was a distant memory. Our vessel was built for the Western Ocean.

With a Mersey pilot embarked, the red ship cleared Eastham Channel. On our port side, we passed a power station and later a dry-dock; to starboard, two Liverpool cathedrals kept vigil – watching over the historic City of Liverpool and its waterfront. The famous liners of yesteryear were long gone; and in their place our red container ship was underway in the night. Passing New Brighton pier, the Liverpool cityscape began to fall astern. At the Bar Light Float our Mersey pilot gave us a hearty wave and 'bon voyage'; our next pilot would speak with a distinctive French-Canadian intonation, and advise ship's officers as we faced the mighty St Lawrence River. Before that final journey into the heart of North America, we must safely cross the windswept North Atlantic. We were Western Ocean men, prepared for the weather and other hazards of the merciless sea.

We had seen on our futuristic horizon the promise of satellite navigation; but in the 1970s we depended on traditional position fixing: terrestrial three bearing fix and Decca navigation in coastal waters; then we employed our celestial navigation skills when crossing the ocean, if the sky and the sea horizon were both clear enough; plus, the skills of working up an Estimated Position, closely related to a Dead Reckoning position (DR). To quote author Charles H. Cotter,

In navigation, a DR position is a position on the navigator's chart worked up from the last observed position, and makes no allowance for current or leeway… then, to this DR position is added the estimate for disturbing factors including current. Such

a final position is known as the Estimated Position (EP). The EP is the most reliable position obtainable without new observations of celestial or terrestrial objects.

Whatever our position fixing method, in the summer season we set our Great Circle course for bleak Belle Isle Strait, a stretch of water between northern Newfoundland and the wild Canadian mainland coast of Labrador. A summer iceberg alleyway. At times, we made our voyage to Belle Isle with the sun, moon and stars out of sight due to cloud cover throughout. North Atlantic grey skies day after day. In reality, with only Estimated Positions to aid our best navigation effort, we often made a Newfoundland landfall with great accuracy – being only a few nautical miles in error, after crossing an entire ocean east to west.

Weather reports and ice reports proved to be a key feature to a safe sea passage, because in winter or summer the forces of nature could unite against a red ship on this great ocean. The Atlantic was usually rough, very rough or so rough that we needed to heave-to, steering head to wind to ride out the storm. We have witnessed the barometric pressure fall so low, that the needle fell off the bottom scale of our barograph cylinder. The wind would howl like the Banshee, and we found ourselves in seas best described as phenomenal/mountainous, with waves 30 metres high, causing at times such violent ship motion that sailors were thrown from their bunks. Given this reality, seasoned sailors do not love the sea; respect is the word. To a North Atlantic seaman, the grey mist on the sea's face; the calm before the storm; the hazards of hurricane and ice all form the background to the working day. Before I signed on for my first Manchester – Montreal voyage, a Master Mariner I knew from my BP days commented on my forthcoming voyages. He simply said, 'Rather you than me'.

Western Ocean voyages were not all in discomfort however, and as soon as watchkeeping was established, life could become very tolerable. Some found time to make models; some watched films or made music; some read or studied. There was always good food and 1970s silver service in the Officers' Mess (in the 21st Century this would become self-service catering). Sailors' talk was often of disaster, or near disaster (worse things happen at sea). Sleep was adequate, providing you could wedge yourself in during a Storm Force 10. Northern weather could also be very warm and kind; wives who accompanied husbands would sit out in the sun on these out-of-character days. But the sun had more use to the mariner than providing a tan.

Back to navigation. Officers liked the routine of 'shooting' the morning and meridian sun, when possible, to work up an accurate daily noon observation, which was transferred daily to the crew track-chart. Likewise, during evening twilight, the Chief Officer took pride in using Polaris (The Pole Star) and other stars and planets to provide a fix on the chart before nightfall. During each watch the duty OOW would also seek to check compasses, using an observation (azimuth) of the sun, moon or stars. As the 2000hrs–midnight OOW, I always tried to use the star Arcturus for my evening compass check. (A 21st Century comment: as technology has taken over, navigation routines have been sidelined by other routines dominated by satnav and other high-tech innovation. Progress is progress. We may reach a stage when unmanned ships take the place of men and women sailing with whales and dolphins for company. A sad thought perhaps?).

Our red ship sailed onwards to make good her westerly course. Longitude thirty degrees west, forty degrees west, fifty degrees west. Canada was ever closer; our BBC radio faded away; the chimes of Big Ben were overtaken by other voices. At breakfast time, the Canadian DJ would bid us good morning with a road traffic report for Newfoundland drivers. He would tell listeners to take care on the highway and issued birthday greetings to someone's husky. The book of life fell open at the North American page. Welcome to Canada. North America is a vast landmass, and after clearing Newfoundland coastal waters we continued our westward journey towards Montreal and the Canadian heartland. We were surrounded by the tidal waters of the Gulf of the St Lawrence. In the winter season, pack ice dominated the route; but ships built for Canadian winters made steady progress through the ice, with strengthened hulls and marine engines designed with power for the task. Our red ships were rarely subject to delays caused by ice.

We entered the St Lawrence River and embarked our first river pilot at the Les Escoumins pilot station. (The 2022 web page reads: 'On April 8, 1960, the pilot station was moved to a site on the North Shore of the St Lawrence: the wharf at Les Escoumins). Those local pilots worked their patch, the lower St Lawrence, and advised vessels during the first inbound leg as far as Québec City; here pilots changed as we progressed inland towards Montreal. Some views were pure wilderness; some views were highways with massive trucks; some views were riverside homes. The Québec cityscape was remarkable with the sight of weathered bright green copper roofs. Separatist issues dominated the political landscape of Québec Province during the 1970s, and this subject was never far away during officers' banter with St Lawrence River pilots, plus the local tax burden of the 1976 Montreal Olympic Games. (I managed a free entry to a diving event).

At Trois-Riviéres (Three Rivers) the river pilots changed for the last part of the journey. As the new pilot added his name to the Deck Logbook we could see Lac St Pierre ahead, and then Sorel; finally, we made our approach to the container terminal at Montreal. On arrival, we needed to survey and repair any damage from the Atlantic crossing. (One of my tasks on arrival was to record the ship's draught fore and aft; and on one memorable occasion the ship was 'down by the head' – caused by seawater ingress. Salt water present in the forepeak, caused by hull damage near the bow, according to the survey. This meant welders at work during our busy 24/7 cargo work operation, to preserve seaworthiness on the return voyage to the UK. All in a day's work.) We had survived our ocean crossing; we had enjoyed a safe passage inland via the St Lawrence; depending on the season, we marvelled at the forest colours of red, orange and yellow during autumn or the full-curtained wonder of Aurora Borealis.

By way of contrast on arrival, a short bus ride into down-town Montreal offered a few hours respite from our ship routine. The city was dominated by typical North American skyscrapers, by Mount Royal and by the Olympic Stadia. The Hudson Bay Company also operated a downtown store as big as an Indian reservation. There was much to see. Meanwhile, alongside a more functional construction of concrete, cranes and tarmac, the red ship discharged her cargo and then loaded containers for the UK. The whole active operation ran 24/7 and was dominated by the speed of cargo work. Finally, we heard the loud crash of hatch covers being secured. Soon we gave the order for crew to proceed to harbour stations. A fresh river pilot embarked and we bade farewell to Montreal. More grey skies; more ice and more Atlantic storms. We quietly left Canada astern. Our red ship would soon return to Montreal with another crew.

The North Atlantic confirmed that all human life was at sea: the unsung heroes of the Western Ocean: Masters, Mates and Marine Engineers; Able Seamen, engine-room greasers, cooks and stewards; occasional rouges, scoundrels and pier-head-jumpers. All homeward bound – like generations of seafarers before us. Éire's Fastnet light 'loomed up' on the port bow; the hills of Ireland rolled into the sea. Liverpool, Manchester, make fast. Secured in home port. Train to family – warm greetings. The laughter of my children, plus their games and their singing. Their smiles were always brighter than the stars in the northern sky.

Tall Ships: Years to come
– Author aloft, 1989 – 2015.

Two years service on regular North Atlantic voyages, together with my years of BP sea-training, gave me a well-rounded experience of the UK's Merchant Navy. I was always determined not to become an absent father; so, when I returned to 'shoreside' employment in 1978, I thought that might be the end of my seafaring days. Life would turn out to be quite the opposite. The remaining pages of my narrative cover my mid-life honours degree – supported by cable ship operations across the world, and my venture into leadership training. Plus, a 25-year seagoing project: my deck officer voyages in sail training ships until my 70th year. UK Tall Ships would provide a final big challenge and my end-game. My memory of an albatross flying above angry waves would continue to inspire.

Bright-Remembered Western Ocean
In my mind I recapture a moment of time
When the sunlight and waves interwove
Where Guardian Ailsa Craig rose from the sea
And a ship and her burden sailed westwards with me.

In my mind I restructure a moment of time
When a gannet aloft in the dawn
Unleashed by the impulse that throbbed in its heart
Sea-dived from the sky like a white feathered dart.

In my mind I remember a moment of time
When the growlers and 'bergs of Belle Isle
Were kissed by the light of a Labrador sky
White sentinelled passage – Red Ships passing by.
Peter John Hill, 1998.

Chapter 9

Essential Time Ashore with My Own Dear Children

Halcyon Family Days, 1980.
Siblings: Watercolour by Janette Hill, with Brian and Brent.

I have taken my global seafaring in dramatic bursts, followed by a season of normal domestic family life. During my North Atlantic adventures in red ships, hurricane force winds, angry seas and ice, the sea bestowed its best gifts: a sense of camaraderie, rewarding professional work and robust health. These seafaring blessings would generally remain with me throughout the following years – certainly until I elected to retire from the sea aged 69 years in 2015.

In 1978, after two years in the North Atlantic service with Manchester Liners, I then completed my second major phase at sea, engaged in financially rewarding work in the North Sea oil fields, working as a tanker deck officer, bringing in cargoes of crude oil, from the Beryl oilfield into a Thames refinery. It was big-ship work, with little or no drama after the savage North Atlantic. However, during my short North Sea interlude, I was able to facilitate a sea rescue, going to the aid of the wife of a ship's engineer, during one dramatic embarkation from our anchorage in the Firth of Forth. The weather was wild Scottish wind and rain.

This 1978 rescue involved simple instinctive action on my part; it resulted in a young life saved according to her husband. His ship-visiting wife was on our pilot ladder leaving our 80,000 tonne North Sea tanker, shrouded in darkness. I was already in the small liberty boat attending alongside, many metres below the high embarkation gate. We were helping ship visitors as they disembarked via the vertical pilot ladder and the very lively liberty boat. There was a big swell running which caused the liberty boat to rapidly rise and fall through 4 or 5 metres, up and down the ship's side. With the visiting wife over the side on the ladder, the liberty boat fell away with the swell; then it pitched us up the ship's side at a rate of knots towards the slim young wife. She was vulnerable and in our rapidly ascending flight-path. As our small boat rose to knock her off into the wine-dark sea, I was able to remain firm-footed on deck as I literally snatched her from the pilot ladder as we raced into her precarious position. As the liberty boat then fell rapidly away, I hung on to our visitor, avoiding falling off balance. All's well that ends well. Seafaring is full of rapidly worsening situations such as this. Instinctive action – no heroics. Right place; decisive response. No tears.

My interval in the North Sea involved many incidents of leaving my ship in heavy weather to go ashore on ship's business or to go on leave. It was after another stormy disembarkation, that I sought the comfort of my home and family for a while. I was then offered a shore-based appointment solving more industrial storage and material handling problems. With three growing children, it seemed a very good idea at the time. But this latest shoreside venture, which began in 1978, would end in personal grief and further major life choices. More learning curves on my radar. Yet again, I would need to recall that giant wandering albatross in the southern seas. The image of that heroic seabird had a lifelong impact. A further period of personal survival was just a handful of years away, as I was handed keys to another brand-new company car, blissfully unaware of mountains left to climb. And oceans still to cross. Fast forward to dark 1981.

In reality, my seafaring days were far from over. I would eventually be making regular voyages in the UK fleet of Tall Ships – but even in the early 1980s this was still over my horizon. The 1980s saw life-changing events across the UK.

1978 to 1981 were prosperous years ashore for us as a family unit, even with the UK economy beginning to wobble. It was the calm before the storm of a national meltdown in economic activity, otherwise known as a major recession.

My UK Tall Ships' Future: 1989–2015.

There would be no more well-paid hiding places either ashore or away at sea. A major rethink would be required to support my long-term survival in employment.

I had picked up the threads of shore-based industrial project activity in 1978 and everything worked out very well through to mid-1982. My North Atlantic/North Sea sojourn had yielded renewed health and fitness, and I had regained my old levels of confidence and organising ability. As a family, we also moved from our refurbished property on Tyneside, back to the welcoming pastures of rural Worcestershire. Our children moved from old inner-city schools on Tyneside to a village school near Evesham Road Ridgeway, Astwood Bank: within sight of the distant Malvern Hills. It was all a breath of fresh air. Our new garden began to flourish. As with any family, the new and unforeseen happened to us, as it always does. During the winter of 1979, I had a close shave during a road traffic accident. No other vehicle was involved, but I hit a patch of ice on a country lane early one winter's morning. The car rolled over as I listened to Richard Baker's classical selection on the car radio. I can recall every detail of that slow-motion road traffic incident; but as the roof caved in above my head, I remained secured by my seat belt and uninjured. A passing driver stopped and came to my aid, switching off the ignition as he opened the driver's door. I crawled out with only a scratch on my nose. Delayed shock followed – nothing more than a blue-light ambulance ride, followed by a quiet two-hour recovery in a cottage hospital. The car was written off – perhaps a sign of things to come in my working life.

The UK economy was also about to make a casualty of my latest industrial venture. But, for the time being a replacement car was delivered to my door. For a while, my own work thrived amidst the economic downturn. In 1981, I won a company competition by producing high financial results in my section of the company's own 'beat the economic gloom' initiative. The prize was a newly-launched British Leyland 'Metro' car, with keys presented at a gala event fronted by the British actress Joanna Lumley. This bright remembered event left me with two cars; it also sets in context the contrasting 'Dear John' company letter dated November 1982: 'You must now clear your desk'. The 1980s UK recession hit me straight between the eyes. The company letter concluded, 'You failed to meet your most recent financial targets…' For a while I was crushed by these events. I was in my early 30s; significant mortgage; family of five. What next? Time for a radical rethink and a clear survival strategy. Time to think about further training? Even a degree? Back to full-time education with a set of clear objectives in mind? Perhaps. There was no easy solution other than the need to face reality. But I was never abandoned by the grace of God or the kindness of strangers.

Chapter 10

Thoughts of Age – Loneliness and change

There are times in life when you need to dig deep and reach high. You may have faith in your own ability; you may believe in the goodness of God; or you may have confidence in nothing. At times, any confidence can be severely tested. You may look for rhyme and reason in life and find a brick wall. For a while, nothing makes any sense, and you can find yourself occupying a very dark and lonely place. A short-term plan was needed as I saw the reality of my long-term situation; I was still young and was hopeful of productive working years ahead; so, I faced the immediate issues and worked out a reduced payment scheme with our family mortgage provider; I also 'signed on' and was awarded whatever UK state benefits my situation allowed. I then set to work doing two things: writing letters seeking work; and I also embarked on household maintenance to keep myself occupied on a daily basis. Practical problems call for positive action.

My letters included over 40 applications to well-known shipping companies. Most replied – explaining that the severe recession meant no plans for hiring more seafaring staff. The job market was in meltdown across the UK by New Year 1983. Therefore, after much soul-searching, I decided to enrol on a higher education course to begin in October 1983 at a regional college (which became The University of Worcester). I had no Advanced level qualifications: but my former nautical college gave me an academic reference based on past grades. As a result, when it came to my college interview for a full degree programme, I was offered an unconditional place. I was aware that I was all set to spend four years as a full-time student – as I also hoped to qualify as a graduate maths teacher. There would be a long slog ahead; and life would never be the same for Elaine, my wife – who, to her credit, went out and began her own demanding part-time work. Between us, we established a strong survival team; but there were grave doubts expressed, even before I set foot on my degree ladder in 1983.

A deep searching question was put to me by a serving college Principal. I was introduced by a family friend, and went along to discuss the academic challenge I faced. At the end of a long conversation in his office, he simply asked – how would I survive a four-year course with a mortgage and three children, even with a government grant and a part-time income from my wife? It was a fair question. I had a new Volvo car, plus some savings to help us through. However, there was concern that my degree plans might not work out. The next four years would be another major learning curve for the whole family; but the years were destined to end in academic success. My hard-won honours degree would transform the rest of my professional life, and also expand my global seagoing experience well beyond my limited imagination. There was no way of knowing it, but another adventure lay ahead. Therefore, October 1983 arrived, and I became a mature student; but not without honest misgivings from my first day on campus.

I can recall every moment of that 1983 enrolment day for my degree. I arrived early in my shiny new Volvo, wearing polished shoes, a white shirt and tie – dressed for the business. Suddenly, I found myself alone in the Freshers' Hall surrounded by excited young people in jeans, waving their UK 'A level' results. Teenage aspirations and straight from Sixth Form. I looked in vain for soulmates – other mature students with rich life experience. I could find none. Not one face appeared to be over 18. I walked away, got into my car and parked in central Worcester where I made for a coffee shop, sat down and re-examined my life and my options. I sat in a daze for about two hours, and finally decided that I had very limited options at that moment in time. I went back to the college and signed up. It was an autumn 1983 decision that I have never regretted. Not that my first year as an undergraduate was a walk in the park. I had signed on to struggle. I rapidly came to see the merit of wrestling with any degree course. And I eventually discovered other mature students struggling with the same issues as myself and my family. The next four years would be a true learning curve and provide rich rewards. The four-year journey would also be a worthwhile venture in its own right. But one step at a time; work to short-term objectives when you are in a fix, with responsibility for home and family. By Christmas 1983, I was well into my studies. And I gave it everything. By the spring of 1984, I was playing tennis with other students and members of the academic staff. Never a great tennis player: Love – Forty. But I was enjoying the journey. My spirit soared.

However, my first academic year ending June 1984 would finish with great stress and disappointment. I was getting good grades overall; but not in my key maths programme. Maths and physics had been my strong points as an officer at sea. Why was I struggling with the subject now? But this was far from trig ratios and spherical triangles. I was into unknown territory, and only just about holding my own. I passed all the pure maths coursework set during that first year. But much of it was a challenge; and all of it was so-called New Mathematics. For the first time in my life, I really was struggling – with statistics, probability, calculus and the rest. The lack of studying pure maths at Advanced level was my weakness.

So, it came to the June 1984 exam season. My course also involved studies in economics and education theory, and I passed both courses in the June exams. I also passed my final pure maths coursework; but had an undisputed fail grade in the June maths exam paper. My retake in September 1984 yielded a similar result – which meant that I had blown away my first year. This was a real setback. Having spent the entire summer revising for the September 1984 retake – only to be confronted with recurring failure troubled me. This would take some sorting out. Overall failure was not part of my plan. The situation was not easy to digest. The college however, via the good intervention of the Vice Principal, offered me a fresh start on a three-year course: BA (Hons) in Combined Studies. I was very reluctant to begin again from day one; but, after discussing the options with my wife Elaine, a decision was made to accept the offer of a second attempt at academic success. So, we threw caution to the wind; and the first positive thing I did was land a short-term role at sea, sailing as Relief Mate in a UK based coastal ship.

The vessel was engaged in dredging in the Solent for construction industry aggregate. A humble rust-bucket of a ship with a crew of seven; but it was an important appointment for me. As a result, I quickly regained my sea legs before returning to a new opportunity at Worcester to kick-start my higher education ambitions. Of equal importance, the small step of a 1984 short appointment at sea would pave the way to a whole series of well-paid seafaring contracts to support my fresh degree studies. Looking back years afterwards, I realised that my later series of vacation contracts from 1985, all in the marine world of sub-sea cable projects, would prove to be a once in a lifetime event. I would eventually be flying off to all points of the compass to support my degree studies and keep my family finances secure. Small steps; big strides. Never bid farewell to hope. The summer of 1984 was to prove a major turning point in my adult life and attitude. My future sub-sea cable work as a deck officer would also become my direct route to 25 years of regular voyages as an officer in UK Tall Ships – through to 2015. Never give up. I have learned to be bold in life – take the opportunities as they appear on your radar. Keep a sharp eye on working to make things happen. You fall off your bike. Dust down and soldier on. Learn to soar above the threatening waves. It is the albatross factor. The Kipling factor… on the pathway to some kind of coping maturity.

If you can fill the unforgiving minute
With sixty seconds' worth of distance run
Yours is the Earth and everything that's in it
And – which is more – you'll be a man, my son.
Rudyard Kipling

Not PC in 2022 I know, but Kipling makes for some good reading.

Chapter 11

BA (Hons) Degree: Ships are Alright – Hidden treasure

Following the dramatic dark cloud of the summer of 1984, I made my fresh academic start and quickly rekindled a positive learning mode. At times, we must accept defeat and struggle to come up with a new plan. It pays us to learn something from the darkest experience. Learn never to fear failure. Find the strength to advance, even on days of severe pressure. I would discover fresh encounters with kind strangers. Through triumph and disaster: *Amazing Grace*.

Therefore, in October 1984, I began a three-year full-time course which would be successful and result in the award of my BA honours degree in June 1987. My final 2.1 honours grade was supported by my final year dissertation entitled *Character Development*. My wife would eventually attend my graduation, with me 'in absentia'. I would be in the USA based in Baltimore Harbour serving in the UK cable ship *Mercury*. I would phone home from Washington DC to obtain a family report of my missed graduation. I will now set before the reader the remarkable events leading to my eventual success story. Not only did I enjoy my BA undergraduate experience; I also completed (in college vacations) some of the most interesting work of my career in the Merchant Navy – in European seas, the North Atlantic and the Pacific Ocean. This remarkable part of my story unfolds below. After my graduation, Tall Ships' deployment would become a key feature of my work. My 1987 graduation would influence the rest of my working days. I would eventually retire in 2015, qualified as MCA Chief Mate in Tall Ships.

It is not my intention to dwell on the minutiae of my BA degree studies, except to highlight my final year BA dissertation research. The subject followed me on my seaman's flight to Fiji during July 1986. It flew out of Heathrow in the form of a newspaper feature on my first leg to Los Angeles – and somehow arrived in Fiji with me courtesy of Air New Zealand. The critical newspaper article was a feature based on the life and educational philosophy of Kurt Hahn, a German born educator and founder of Gordonstoun School. The whole experiential learning philosophy of Kurt Hahn would prove to be the final jewel in the crown of my undergraduate studies. It is important to keep in mind my initial academic struggle during that first challenging year in 1983. Exam failure in my first year was raw; but several positive aspects paid dividends, because by summer 1984 I had at least developed the skill of producing academic essays on many subjects.

Read; attend lectures; participate in seminar groups; make notes; develop a fluid writing style; attend one-to-one tutorials. In short, develop a personal academic style and refine it as you progress. I was seasoned, ready and primed by October 1984. Early failure served me very well overall. As an experienced academic student, I managed to sail through the calm waters of my first year of my BA honours programme. In addition, my demanding seafaring contracts from 1985 onwards were all well rewarded; these contracts explain how my family survived my four student years without us sinking into hardship and any debt burdens.

In keeping with my overall theme of seafaring throughout life, it is important therefore to explain how I came to be on a long flight to Fiji in the summer of 1986. It all began during the 1985 summer vacation of my BA degree course, when I was introduced to the engineering marvels of a large European sub-sea cable laying operation (as a forerunner to my 1986 flight to Fiji). My new dawn.

This 1985 situation involved a summer opportunity as a student, which would provide the re-commencement of professional contracts and major earned income at sea, thanks to the intervention of a 500-year-old British nautical institution known as Trinity House. I cannot stress enough the significance of an interview conducted by Captain Dove: a fellow officer employed by Trinity House, based in Harwich. With the stroke of his pen offering me a contract of summer employment, Captain Dove (as a total stranger) changed the rest of my seafaring days to 2015. The outcome of my 1985 job interview with Trinity House was really as dramatic as that. The kindness of strangers indeed. For the duration of the 1985 summer college vacation, I was to join Trinity House (Dioptric Division) as a company Second Officer, working a two week on/two week off sea roster.

It was a perfect opportunity, at that moment in my life, for my family and also for my degree course. But first, I was required to report to Dover in July 1985 and join a Trinity House vessel deployed in the busy shipping lanes of the English Channel. My role was to support a 24/7 radar surveillance operation, while two cable ships laid power cables across the seabed between Folkstone and a French terminal beach-head south of Calais. Our prime mid-channel task was to prevent collisions between congested shipping using the Dover Strait and the cable laying vessels moving slowly across those shipping lanes. It was a complex operation with a reported budget of £700,000,000 in 1985. The managers had direct communications into the heart of Government on both sides of the English Channel. There were four sub-sea Channel cables, each designed to facilitate the transfer of power between national grids to cope with different peak-power demands. A massive engineering project to enable a light bulb in Folkstone to function with French electricity. *Entente Cordiale.*

In every way, 'Operation Channel Cable' was a mega high-octane project which included a large trenching vehicle on the seabed manned by French divers. During my tours there were many close encounters with vessels posing a threat to the cable ships. Frequent daily use of Channel 16 VHF marine radio was made, as we warned vessels to keep clear of our buoyed sea-patch measuring two square nautical miles. Newly developed shipboard ARPA radars were a feature on our operational platform; it was our task as Trinity House officers to make a positive ID of radar shipping targets posing a threat, and then contact them by VHF to facilitate early and substantial action, and thereby to create sea-room between the seagoing threat and our slow sub-sea cable operation. There were some difficult moments when very large ships ignored both our clear VHF radio warnings, and our many signal-rocket warning shots. Literally, rockets shot across the bows of threatening ships. If totally ignored, our fragile guardships would then proceed to approach and force an alteration of course by the offending vessel. After two weeks of close encounters and our full-on radar surveillance, Trinity House officers (including the author) were ready for two weeks paid shore leave. It was a very challenging deployment. Surrounded by the marine chaos involved, I managed to sleep soundly when off duty. But my life jacket was always at hand. Any collision could sink our fragile guardship.

There were some very experienced seafarers engaged on the Channel Cable project in 1985, including several very experienced Trinity House Commanders. The OIC of the French cable ship was the former sailing Master of the world-renowned research vessel *Calypso*, owned and run by Jacques Cousteau – the French oceanographer. I was in good company. This single seagoing deployment later motivated my 1986 application to Cable and Wireless (Marine), the leading British company running commercial cable ships. I explained that I was a full-time mature student who had gained experience of marine cable operations as a Trinity House Second Officer during 1985. As a result of my letter and an interview at HQ, in the summer of 1986 Cable and Wireless sent me out to join their vessel *Pacific Guardian*, based in Suva harbour, Fiji. My ongoing financial issues were to be resolved as a result of an application initiated by my work on Operation Channel Cable. Cable and Wireless would, in fact, provide me with many contracts, taking me beyond graduation and well into 1988. The combined grace of God and the kindness of strangers has never let me down. But, other life-shaping decisions were taking place behind the scenes in my family life.

Just before my 1985 summer work with Trinity House, I was offered a full-time well-paid management role; plus, a company car and all the trimmings. All very tempting. The offer came out of the blue, and was made by a good friend who was Chairman of the company making the offer of full-time work. However, it meant abandoning my degree for the commercial challenge of a new logistics business linked to European road haulage. It was to be full-time employment and offered immediate security for my wife and family. I gave it my heartfelt consideration; and with the full backing of my wife Elaine, I decided to finish my honours degree, little knowing that (after Channel Cable) Cable and Wireless would roll out the carpet starting with my Fiji deployment. My own good fortune and subsequent history endorsed the choice I made at that 1985 point in my life. We never know what life has in store, sometimes just a heartbeat away. At times, our fragile human life makes progress based on a simple choice. This has been my experience throughout life; many life issues came into focus after observing as a youth, the flight of the lone albatross in that far-off southern sea. The whole of my mid-life degree was to be supported by ongoing challenging sea-service.

In keeping with the theme of this narrative, my seafaring contracts with Cable and Wireless deserve further mention. As indicated, Fiji 1986 was the first of many contracts. It all began at the end of my second year on my BA honours programme in the summer of 1986. The first thing to arrive on my doormat after the Cable and Wireless job interview was a British Airways return ticket to the South Pacific. Fiji required full tropical preps. In July 1986, I arrived in a taxi at Heathrow Airport to board my first Boeing 747 flight: to Los Angeles on the first leg of a journey to the far side of the world. I would join a ship I had never seen and work with people I had never met before. And this was all part and parcel of my memorable mature student experience. The sheer joy of those days of student sea-contracts would remain with me for a lifetime. Those days were the British Merchant Navy at its best, before the sad days of subsequent decline (British Officers later sailing under Flags of Convenience). However, I will allow positive

Diving Ops: Operation Channel Cable, 1985.

days to prevail as I look back. Fiji was a great success and also provided me with a solid dissertation research project to bring back to the UK. Back to 1986 and the reason for my flight to Fiji to join the cable ship *Pacific Guardian*.

Cable and Wireless had laid the longest fibre optic intercontinental telephone cable of its generation – stretching across the Pacific Ocean from New Zealand via Hawaii to the west coast of North America – to a landfall in British Columbia. Thousands of nautical miles of painstaking engineering via deep sub-sea trenches and submerged mountain ranges, all surveyed beforehand. (The deepest cables in the world can be found miles below the ocean surface). In the event of a cable repair, a specialist cable ship was deployed. That was the assigned role of the ship I joined in Suva, Fiji in the summer of 1986. The vessel had a permanent base in Suva, and a 5,000 nautical mile operational radius, with British officers; Fijian nationals sailed as crew. It was a historic arrangement for the highly professional officers who welcomed me on board after my 27-hour trip from Heathrow (short delays in Los Angeles and Honolulu on the way). This was life at sea as I had never witnessed it; and never seen it since. My fellow officers were in Fiji on two-year tours of duty – with company houses ashore; many had their wives and children living in Fiji. Our Captain had his own corps of ex-pats who met on a regular basis for Morris dancing sessions. This was different. This was a cable ship; but there was also serious training to be done.

Ship's business was indeed to be done in Suva, but in a very laid-back fashion, in keeping with the character of a tropical paradise, as I soon discovered. The ship remained on 24/7 standby for Pacific Ocean cable repairs. As soon as the maroon went up it would be full on – all hands to the pump. In the meanwhile, it was a ship routine conducted at anchor, with liberty boats running throughout the day. All part of the local scene, and employing many local seafarers in a very ex-colonial setting. As I would discover, Fijians not only honoured our Queen; they are the toughest and most cheerful group of people you could wish to meet. The local greeting is 'Bula' – a friendship greeting carrying a feeling of general goodwill. I would get to know the locals well enough. After my arrival and the usual safety briefings, I was informed that the harbour routine would be two days of 24-hour ship duty (Officer of the Day) followed by two days off (Liberty Days). I could live with that. I quickly learned that the Welsh Rugby squad was in town on tour, using the same hotel and pool where I spent much of my regular two days of liberty from ship duty. I was to be surrounded by good cheer and goodwill in a Pacific Ocean setting. The weeks flew past. During my two months tour of duty, I would also find supportive Christian friendship in Suva, swim in a jungle pool, play tennis, play golf and attend a Fijian weekend camp. My main contacts ashore were yacht-owning Kiwi grandparents and a Major in the Fijian army, who was

Author as OOW: Pacific Guardian, 1986.

Evidence: Pacific sharks in abundance, 1986.

Cable ship Pacific Guardian: Fiji, 1986.

also a member of The Great Council of Chiefs. I found myself in good genial company throughout. My yacht owning contacts would later visit my home in the UK; Major Penaia would later contact me from his London hotel.

One bizarre seagoing duty surfaced before our 1986 cable repair exercise in the Pacific Ocean. At our anchorage in Suva harbour, the ship hosted an annual Miss Fiji Business Pageant, when a floodtide of local young female execs attended a reception aboard *Pacific Guardian*, accompanied by an army of chaperones to look after them. It was all done with very high levels of security and general goodwill, as Miss Fiji Banking and others did their best to show keen interest in the hi-tech wonders of a complex cable ship at anchor. Many wives were also in attendance to keep a weather-eye on event proceedings. It may read like a British 1960s comedy film script; but this was all about local public relations.

My 1986 deck officer's berth also involved me serving as Ship's Doctor with keys to the surgery and walk-in times for reviewing seafaring aches and pains. When I was presented with any problem beyond first-aid, I simply arranged for the Fijian seaman to seek qualified medical opinion ashore. I survived my brief clinical career without serious incident. My first Cable and Wireless encounter ended with the long flight back to the UK. Fiji was an insight into ocean cable projects, without any operational deep-sea cable repairs during that first tour of sea duty. My Cable and Wireless contracts after 1987 graduation would involve repairs to U.S. Atlantic cables, Bermuda deployment, Atlantic hurricanes and an encounter with a gun-toting American sailor. Plus, a serious local Fire Service rescue – from the hold of a cable ship in dry-dock, during a ship refit on Tyneside.

However, in October 1986, after I arrived home from the South Pacific, there was still the small matter of my degree to finish. I quickly signed on for my final year of study, and set to work writing my dissertation, based on the educational feature which accompanied my flight from Heathrow to Fiji. The feature made many references to the educational philosophy of Kurt Hahn. So, I gave my dissertation the title *Character Development*. It would lead me eventually to fresh fields of UK education and training, including partnership work with officers of a UK police force; it would also lead to my own development of a UK higher education leadership programme. All detailed in subsequent chapters.

My seaman's BA honours dissertation would also lead me into the orbit of the UK Sail Training Association; and this new link would open the door to 25 years of regular Tall Ships' service between 1989–2015: in UK coastal waters and far beyond. I was destined to eventually sail as an officer in seven UK sail training ships, voyaging as far as the Canaries, Azores, Balearics and Italy. My 1983 option to begin academic study in early middle life, supported by many contracts in distant seas, was about to produce a host of new adventures. Bula. Bon voyage.

Sail training from 1989: Author as Watch Officer.

UK Sail training brig Prince William, 2004.

Chapter 12

Beyond 1987 – A Tall Ship and a star to steer her by

I will now recall some details to my final year of study ending July 1987, and my rewarding sub-sea cable ship projects up to 1988. The overall objective of my degree course was to provide, in middle life, a working platform for the future. My wife and I have looked back on the entire project as a real engaging and transformational time, supported by my worldwide contracts at sea. I have to acknowledge our good fortune: the constant flow of cable ship contracts at just the right time was a once-in-a-lifetime opportunity which, as I shall recall, continued beyond my graduation in 1987. The grace of God and the kindness of strangers were ongoing themes. Without seafaring income, we could have spent years wrestling with a huge debt burden after my degree. It did not happen. Sometimes, success in projects is just being in the right place at the right time.

The remaining narrative therefore indicates the successful end to my experience as a BA student in 1987 (with some detail of final ocean cable ship work) through to my appointment to the lecturing staff at North East Worcestershire College (NEWC) in 1988. My work at NEWC then included my first voyages in UK Tall Ships during 1989 – and moves on to my award (by the UK Maritime and Coastguard Agency) as Chief Mate in September 2001. I would eventually leave NEW College, add to my Tall Ships' seafaring, and then finally retire from the sea in 2015. Between 1987 and 2015 there is, therefore, significant detail to recall. First, I will outline the results of my honours dissertation from 1987. I will deal with the key points.

My 1987 final year BA honours dissertation opens with the following overview:

Character Development: Dissertation submitted by P.J. Hill. Final year academic research project for the award of BA (Hons) Combined Studies (April 1987).
Dissertation Abstract: My honours degree dissertation is concerned with the concept of human character. The early pages require a search for a definition of the term. The conceptual flavour is distilled and finally transformed into a working theoretical model. The term character is delimited into three domains:

1. The Psychological Domain
2. The Ethical Domain
3. The Experiential Domain

This working model was then used throughout the study as the basis for further analysis. The key theoretical works of Kurt Hahn, Freud, Adler, Peters and Erik Erikson, plus the seafaring writings of Conrad, Masefield and R.H. Dana provided the gravitas. The unchecked character of R.H. Dana's Sea Captain was significant.

In addition to a concern for a conceptual definition of the term character, the study was fundamentally concerned with the theme of character development. The Psychological Domain led to an investigation of Freudian theory. It was concluded that certain Freudian constructs and general notions of character development were mutually exclusive. Further study led to a consideration of the psycho-social theories of Erik Erikson and his concept of ego integration.

The Ethical Domain owed much to the theoretical insights of Adler, plus the observations found in the writing of Joseph Conrad. The record of the American seaman R.H. Dana in his book, *Two Years Before the Mast* (1869), included his masterful account of a long voyage from Boston to California, under the command of a powerful, overbearing Captain. Dana described some scenes of unchecked savage power. Consideration was therefore given to character as defined within the world of human behaviour: within the framework of daily life.

A detailed consideration of ethical behaviour was needed; the educational significance of character development began to emerge. Attention was drawn to the educational thinking of Kurt Hahn and his emphasis on the links between demanding social experience and the development of ethical character. Such philosophy led directly to the founding of the UK Outward Bound movement in 1941. Aberdovey was the first UK centre; and this initiative led to UK Tall Ships.

Outward Bound and Tall Ships' experience were identified as primary agents of character development. (A significant comparison was also made between the experience of a demanding residential Tall Ship voyage and the more limited experience of senior-school dinghy sailing). The author was indebted to 1987 research support: from the retired RN Captain serving as Schooner Director UK Sail Training Association at that time; and, also from Worcestershire County Council managers based at Upton Warren Sailing Centre. A final summary bound together the strands of my 1987 study. Further research was advocated.

There are several key chapters in my 1987 honours dissertation (1st Class grade):

1. Character: A Conceptual Model
2. The Psychological Domain of Freud
3. The Psychological Domain of Erikson
4. The Essential Ethical Domain
5. The Experiential Domain based on field research
6. Summary and Conclusions (The above led to BA Hons 2.1 overall).

The Bibliography is extensive, ranging from texts on human development, moral philosophy, classical writers, psychologists, ethical behaviour and various academics and teachers. Several significant conclusions are reached, as follows.

The concept of ego integration comes from Eriksonian theory; and Erikson suggests the potential for ego integration at every stage in life. As a result of experience, the weak ego integration (character) of yesterday can become the stronger ego integration of today. When character is therefore equated with the Freudian concept of ego (but understood in Eriksonian terms) the development of character is possible within a psychological framework. Demanding social and teamwork experience are both required as key developmental agents – and lead to an understanding of the educational philosophy of Kurt Hahn. Outward Bound is considered to have high significant potential; challenging seagoing experience is also on offer: sail training voyages in Tall Ships. Kurt Hahn saw the mountains and the sea as having great potential for character development projects. This was the first significant conclusion of the dissertation. Kurt Hahn made this comment, 'No human being should be compelled into opinions; but it is negligent not to compel human beings (young people in particular) into experience'. This first conclusion leads to the second major conclusion of my 1987 BA (Hons) study (which in the modern world of soft virtual learning, may be very controversial). My second conclusion therefore reads like this:

Experience may mean young individuals facing up to very difficult or at times dangerous situations. (Hahn advocates some senior school involvement in 'real world' life saving and fire/rescue services). In the face of such experience, individuals find a balance between self-centred interest and group interest. To the academic Adler, such boldness of exposure equates to the development of character. In Adlerian terms, the balance is struck between self-aggrandisement and social feeling. Learning to show real support and compassion for the weaker members of a group, when that group has shared real life challenges, is the kind of project in mind. Learning to reflect on a sense of moral duty is also involved. Character development involves moral, compassionate action over and above self-seeking. As a seaman, the Sail Training Association was seen by the author as a major player in the field of providing adventure voyages; and as a result of the dissertation, such voyages would become part of the author's future for over 25 years from 1989. This is then a clear example of a mid-life degree shaping the future and many outcomes of the working life of a single individual. My degree was rewarding in every sense of the word. The white heat of hard mental graft.

As soon as my dissertation was handed in during May 1987, my own cohort of students began to go their separate ways. My wife and I booked a short trip to France; and I began to unwind from dissertation pressures as I waited for the results to be confirmed. The news was good: I was to graduate with a 2.1 honours degree in Combined Studies, with Education and Training Studies as a main subject (hence my interest in character development). Then, hot off the press, Cable and Wireless HR were on the phone offering me a further contract of employment at sea. I was to fly out to Baltimore, State of Maryland to join the US based cable ship *Mercury* for approximately three months. I would miss my own graduation ceremony in Worcester Cathedral – but employment was my key consideration. So, I set out on another seagoing venture, dusted down my seaman-officer uniform and boarded a flight to Washington DC. It was a one-way ticket; I would be returning to the UK with the ship after deployment in the Western Atlantic. My wife would represent me at my autumn 1987 graduation.

I therefore joined cable ship *Mercury* in Baltimore after flying into Washington (Dulles) Airport in August 1987. It was to prove a very varied deployment including a repair to a sub-sea AT&T cable off the coast of New Jersey, followed by our long visit to Wilmington, North Carolina and a memorable very close encounter with hurricane Emily in Bermuda. Finally, we would face the Atlantic crossing to Tyneside in the UK to arrive in November 1987. I would be home for Christmas after a varied year of academic activity and deployment at sea. 1987 was a very rewarding and memorable year. Back to my Baltimore arrival.

In the 1980s, a modern cable repair ship had a solitary purpose: to be on 24/7 standby in its assigned port location across the world. The crew's function was to respond rapidly to a fault or break in a fibre optic sub-sea cable. Many things could go wrong on the seabed, including a malfunction in repeaters laid down with the original cable to boost signal strength. Breaks in sub-sea cables could also occur due to volcanic activity on the seabed. North American shallow water cables could also be damaged by commercial clam dredging. Executing repairs called for skilful deployment of the cable ship in the correct location, raising the cable to the sea surface and finally using the patient and detailed technical skills involved in the cable repair. A cable ship crew was a close multi-skilled team. I was privileged to serve in this specialist area of fibre-optic ocean engineering. Once 'on station' in the sea area, the duty OOW (my role) was stationed, not on the ship's bridge as normal, but at the bow with remote control of the ship's engines and rudder. The objective of the OOW was to maintain the ship's position 'on station' during the repair. In reality, this meant manually using the remote engine and rudder controls to counter the forces of wind, tidal stream and wave energy, which united together could move the ship away from its position. Like many operations at sea, this was not for the faint-hearted. It was interesting work requiring a high level of concentration. However, in the 21st Century, dynamic station-keeping would come to the aid of specialist vessels – deployed across the oceans of the world. All before my time in 1987.

1987 operation: The primary task before cable recovery was to navigate the ship into a position in the general charted area of the reported fault; and the second task was to raise a heavy 'bight' in the cable to the surface, having first successfully snagged the cable with a deployed grappling hook. This sounds all very time consuming in our high-tech era – when rapid communications were becoming ever more rapid and fortunes changed hands daily across global markets via fibre-optic cables. Our North Atlantic Ocean cable repair enterprise was at the cutting edge of global commerce. But, 20th Century cable repairs at sea were slow. However, in former generations the pace was even slower. In my seaman files, I have an account of ocean cable repairs in an earlier age. All very tongue in cheek. An edited version reads as follows, with the unknown original writer presenting a version of events in the life of a very early cable ship, manned by a crew of shades from a different era. *A day in the life of cable ship Morse.*

Morse lay at anchor, rolling in the swell of a foreign port. The Captain sat playing his beloved accordion; around him his crew of hardy sailors danced to his jolly tune, when suddenly the party mood on deck changed. Mr Mate appeared sporting an air of deep gravity. This weather-beaten cable ship officer came rolling along the deck with his urgent message, and gained the attention of his hearty shipmates. The Mate then informed the Captain that a signal had been spotted ashore which flagged up a cable down, somewhere beyond the far blue horizon. It was suddenly all hands to the pump. The Captain gazed at his merry crew, and pondered the fate that awaited each jack-tar. Life would not be easy; but they had trained hard as they danced each day. It was a critical moment. The canny Sea Captain roused himself with a stiffened upper lip and called for the Chief Engineer. The canny Scot-of-a-Chief answered the call from his coal-hole and received orders to get up a full head of steam. It was suddenly all bells and whistles as the cable ship prepared for rapid deployment, as if the wheels of empire rested on this sole nautical endeavour. The Chief consulted with both his Second and a Junior Engineer; they soon recalled the best way to fire up marine engines. After focused trial and error, they were soon underway and clear of the harbour. They would be away for some time; but there was no opportunity to write letters home. Wives and sweethearts knew it took weeks to locate a marine cable and diagnose faults. Their men were all gallant souls in the service of Empire and would eventually keep loved ones informed. As usual, it took many weary days as the cable ship (using a sturdy grappling hook) tried to snag and hoist the cable. When at last they did haul a cable aboard – no fault was found. Efforts all in vain. A return to port revealed a note on the door of the Marine Superintendent. Humble apologies all round – the fault was on shoreside. Rats had damaged the cable; and all office staff had gone on leave to a remote hill station to share tea and tiffin. Farewell to the Captain – and best wishes to all Jolly Jacks. (Anon) (Edited by the author: a cable ship officer).

To recap: The above work of fiction contains facts about locating deep-sea cables. Even in 1987, the standard method for cable retrieval from the seabed was as follows: the cable ship would proceed at slow speed across the charted location of a damaged cable with a grappling device on the seabed, attached by steel wire rope to the cable ship. A chartroom instrument would monitor rapidly rising tension once the seabed cable was snagged by the sub-sea device. The crews of cable ships may never have danced to the tune of their musical Captain; but snagging the faulty marine cable was the signal for all hands to the pump.

This was the world I became a part of in the late 1980s. My first real operation in September 1987 was in the western Atlantic, off the US coast. We left Baltimore harbour, cleared the inshore waters of Chesapeake Bay and headed north to the coastal waters off New Jersey. Within sight of Atlantic City, we located the damaged sub-sea cable and hauled its considerable weight to the surface, severed the cable, buoyed off the severed end, cut out the damaged section, executed a clinical splice and returned the whole working cable to the deep. Slow mission accomplished. Then we returned to a new US base on the Cape Fear River and remained alongside in Wilmington, North Carolina for some time. Life amidst the local Tar-Heels was to prove very interesting.

Once again, during our operational visit to the Carolinas, Cable ship *Mercury* adopted a harbour routine, which provided time to relax and explore the local area. It was my first real taste of the Southern States and I was impressed with the genuine cultural warmth of life south of the historic Mason-Dixon line, 'deed I do.' I enjoyed the company of a retired US husband and wife with Norwegian roots – who were the first Southerners to invite me home for ice-cream and Southern-raised hospitality. I attended their own evangelical Bible Chapel and helped out in their sporting arena. (Remarkably, these Southern friends had met my wife's uncle, during a private trip to Canada). My new friends operated a youth scheme called AWANA – resembling the Scouting movement, and used for sport and Christian teaching in true US Bible Belt fashion. All very genuine, open and honest. They invited me to speak at their meetings and took me to the beach on occasions to swim with sand sharks. Other Wilmington contacts ran US junior soccer teams and took me clam diving on one occasion. They also kindly took me down to South Carolina for an evening drive. On one occasion, I helped them prepare an apartment to cater for a preacher from up north in remote Pennsylvania, who was driving down for the long weekend. Dr S was a very large man with a very small wife, a huge Chevrolet and enough personal gear in his trunk to last for months on the road. The American way.

Soon, it was farewell to the good folks of Wilmington, North Carolina – and we sailed away to repair a sub-sea cable linking Cuba and Miami; and after that repair, we were ordered to deploy to the naval dockyard in Bermuda. Cable ships were based in some excellent locations. We arrived at the Scorpion's Tail dockyard close to the end of the 1987 hurricane season. As we secured the ship at the naval base the name Emily meant nothing. This was all about to change.

We would remain in Bermuda for three weeks. Towards the end of our quiet stopover on this exclusive island of white houses and coral sands, we received a signal that tropical storm Emily was developing into a full-blown hurricane, sweeping in towards the Caribbean from seas off West Africa. The eye of the system was predicted to bypass Bermuda; we were secure at the naval base. But the best weather forecasters can get it wrong. Their predictions are always based on mathematical models and probability. Royal Navy officers walked aboard in the early hours of 25th September 1987 with a warning that Hurricane Emily had changed track – the eye of the storm would pass over Bermuda. As indeed it did. Emily found us with extra mooring lines out fore and aft. Cable ship *Mercury* was as prepared as any ship unable to proceed at short notice into safer, deep water away from the island. We took the full fury and force of hurricane Emily, moored alongside a concrete jetty with many fenders deployed. No damage to the ship. But the paradise island of Bermuda was torn apart by the fury of Emily.

When it was all over and quiet, I walked around the island to observe the damage. Roofing torn off; large trees uprooted; headstones flattened in local graveyards; boats lifted out of the water like toys. It was a scene of disaster. Thankfully there was little evidence of loss of life. Emily left her own trail of disaster. Wikipedia reports,

Hurricane Emily was a powerful tropical cyclone that struck Hispaniola in September 1987. It was the first hurricane in the Caribbean Sea since Hurricane Katrina of 1981 and had the second-fastest forward speed of a 20th-century hurricane, behind only the 1938 New England hurricane. Emily formed out of a tropical disturbance that moved off the west coast of Africa on Sept 20; the storm quickly attained hurricane status. The storm attained its peak intensity with winds of 125 mph. The storm weakened to Category 2 status before making landfall in the Dominican Republic. Then, after weakening to a tropical storm, Emily rapidly tracked north-eastward through the Atlantic Ocean, undergoing a second phase of rapid intensification before passing directly over Bermuda on September 25, 1987.

The crew of cable ship *Mercury* was thankful that a very close encounter with a North Atlantic hurricane left us with no damage to the ship. Shortly afterwards, our vessel and her experienced crew were deployed again to repair further sub-sea cable damage in the shallow sea off Atlantic City; afterwards we plotted courses for the Western Approaches to the UK. We sailed homewards from American waters and crossed the North Atlantic without further incident.

I was serving as the 12-4 OOW (midnight to 0400hrs; midday to 1600hrs). We were a trusted and experienced group of cable ship officers: although on call 24/7, our Captain was not called to the bridge from leaving US coastal waters to arriving off the Port of Tyne. With dry-dock repairs long planned in the UK, we eventually embarked our North Sea pilot at Brixham. We then joined the congested North East shipping lanes off the coast of France, navigated our passage into the North Sea and arrived at our Tyneside destination for our normal family reunions.

I left the ship in November to spend Christmas 1987 at home with my wife and children. The whole period of sub-sea cable repair techniques had been a new experience for me as a seafarer, embracing fresh seamanship skills. There had been throughout, a very powerful and rewarding mixture of both camaraderie and seamanship, combined with working at the sharp end of sub-sea cable repairs, which was to set me up for two further contracts with Cable and Wireless before moving on to graduate employment ashore. I was thankful of the fact that I had completed my degree and gone immediately into the workplace and a good salary, albeit on a short-term contract basis. It was enjoyable work with the normal professional edge of being a trusted team player. Christmas and New Year quickly passed, and as Easter approached, I was back on a transatlantic flight to re-join my ship. Cable ship *Mercury* was again snug and secure alongside in Baltimore when I embarked. This time I would get to explore the Baltimore area, and gain some further insight into the American psyche. This would prove to be quite dramatic. A version of cable ship *Mercury* 1988 High Noon follows.

It happened on my watch, on a quiet Saturday afternoon in the Delaware River. With a local 'Confederacy' pilot embarked, we were minding our own business underway in a buoyed channel, on passage towards Philadelphia for some repair work. All very normal. A calm, sunny day at sea in sheltered waters. One nautical mile ahead of us, on our starboard bow, was a small ocean-going yacht. I will call her the 'Angry Yankee'. She was a New York vessel; and she was flying the Stars and Stripes – her stern ensign. She was steering the same course as us; and she was also in the main shipping channel, but not restricting our ability to safely navigate our large and elegant cable ship. All was peaceful; but the blissful scene in the calm waters of the Delaware River was about to change. Our pilot decided he did not approve of yachts occupying his main shipping channel. Words were about to be exchanged. The American Civil War was about to resurface. As we overhauled the yacht, our pilot decided to give the crew of the yacht a lecture on courtesy at sea. More of a hectoring Smokey Mountain Sunday sermon from our starboard bridge-wing. The Yankee yachtsman did not appreciate our pilot's fine pulpit tone. He certainly did not take kindly to being referred to as a boy. 'Deed he did not'. There is no other way of reporting the declaration of hostility: the Yankee Yachtsman decided to ram cable ship *Mercury*, and sink us there and then. From his nautical vantage point, we were dead men walking. I am familiar with the term 'Barrister's Bluster'; this was Yankee yachtsman's bluster. As the yacht turned hard-to-port, and aimed its bow at our steel mid-ship plates, the Delaware River incident suddenly became very serious. However, as yacht 'Angry Yankee' missed her large tonnage target and slid quietly into our wake, the angry marine skirmish seemed to be over. But not quite. Our angry Yankee bare-knuckle fighter had only just begun. He got lost somewhere in our wake, and found himself slipping further astern. Perhaps he was watching a John Wayne movie? Who knows? He began calling us repeatedly on VHF Channel 16. Many times, he called; many times, we ignored his call. The final High Noon shout came from yacht 'Angry Yankee'. His memorable words still echo across the water; he simply laid down his challenge to our vessel, 'Why don't you stop your ship? Let's sort this out like men.' We thankfully arrived in Philadelphia for repairs in good health. Somewhere a New York yachtsman is repeating his version of his daring 1988 assault on an English cable ship. O say can you see...?

In contrast to the skirmish at sea, I quickly discovered that Philadelphia could be a city of brotherly love and warm hospitality. Baltimore had been exactly the same. The locals were a pleasure to deal with. I enjoyed warm open Christian friendship and fellowship in all of those Southern States; I was invited to speak in their evangelical meeting halls and churches. I have never forgotten their kindness to a total stranger. I would complete one final contract with Cable and Wireless in that year following my graduation. Like all sub-sea work from 1985 in the English Channel, and the later in the USA, my final contract would also be memorable. I disembarked cable ship *Mercury* in early May 1988 and returned to my home in the UK for a few weeks respite. My break from Conrad's '… endless, obscure contest with the sea'.

My final tour of sea duty in a cable ship began in June 1988. I joined a refit team deployed in a UK shipyard. Having been stationed in Cable and Wireless ships located inside South Pacific coral reefs; in Wilmington, North Carolina; alongside in Bermuda and Baltimore, my final tour was somewhat much less exotic. More 'Jungle' North Shields than Fiji jungle. *Cable Venture* was undergoing a major refit on the North East coast of the UK, in the much less sultry location of Swan Hunter's shipyard, Wallsend on Tyne. When I joined in June 1988, the ship was in such a state that all refit crew were based in a hotel in Whitley Bay, with a daily commute to and from the shipyard. The ship itself had reached a mid-point in its refit contract. She was a daily tangle of scaffold, pipes, steel plates, paint and the general chaos of shipyard life. I had seen it all before in regular dry-docking routines. But this was a major refit before a fibre-optic cable-laying contract across the North Atlantic. Her position was daily major-refit chaos. However, traditional UK shipyards had a habit of transforming apparent chaos into a ship ready to be handed over after sea trials. Order quickly began to take the upper hand; and working officers moved from the hotel into ship's cabins. However, the work in the yard continued 24/7 and I discovered the joy of turning in at night, only to be woken by the sound of the nightshift working in the steel echo-box compartment above my bunk – going hammer and tongs all night. It was so bad on one occasion that I travelled to my in-laws home the next morning, across the Tyne, to get some sleep. Nerves were fraying aboard amongst all ranks. This was an uncomfortable routine to say the least. And, it was to get even worse with a ship incident which almost ended in disaster.

I was one of a group of ship's officers working on different aspects of the refit; we attempted to work as a fine-tuned team, also managing an Officer of the Day (OOD) routine between us. However, approaching the end of the 1988 refit we had engaged a squad of local painting contractors working in the depths of the cargo holds (aka cable tanks on a cable ship). The paint-spraying routine was highly paid hazardous piecework. Chemicals in paints can do very nasty things to human lungs. The painting teams were under orders to take frequent breaks from the job. This requirement appeared, on reflection, to be ignored by teams working for big money in sometimes less than perfect conditions. The reader will begin to get the picture of what was going on at the moment the Chief Engineer came racing to my OOD location in the chartroom with urgent news – men from the painting squad had flaked-out on a tank top, in a cable-tank many metres below the main deck. Overcome by paint fumes. Time to raise the alarm. This

Captured in a calm sea moment: Prince William – one of the Tall Ships I would eventually navigate through bleak Atlantic nights, before retiring in my 70th year.

was a life-threatening situation on a bright summer day in Wallsend. I responded by sounding the General Alarm to evacuate the ship; the shipyard Gatehouse crew made a 999 call to the Northumberland Fire Service.

At least four fire-pumps made a rapid blue-light response with all crews donning BA kit. The situation became a major emergency operation. As the fire-pump crews arrived, I was completing a roll-call on hardstanding next to the ship. As duty OOD, I then met the firefighters as they proceeded towards the ship, giving their own OIC an 'on-the-hoof' incident briefing, and then we led the first party of fully prepared firefighters to the entry point of the cable-tank. I then called in more firefighters, two BA kits at a time, to reinforce the rescue attempt. Finally, after strenuous efforts by the Fire Service rescue teams running up and down ladders, painting contractors were hauled in stretchers to the main deck and taken to hospital. No loss of life. All contractors recovered; and during the following onboard debrief, the on-scene Fire Service Commander presented a working summary of the rescue, and paid a tribute to the contribution made by ship's officers. A good result for all concerned, except for the fact that the report from the hospital indicated that the painting squad had all been dismissed as contractors, even before their eventual full recovery and medical discharge from the hospital. A lesson for all concerned. The successful rescue was an example of cooperation and teamwork. Shortly afterwards, *Cable Venture* finally left Swan Hunters Yard on Tyneside after completing her sea trials between Tynemouth and Blyth. I went home to start a new chapter in life, and eventually begin 25 years of regular sail training voyages. More heart-warming sea stories.

Chapter 13

NEW College – Still the sea in the heart's deep core

After completing my 1988 early summer contract in Swan Hunter's shipyard, Wallsend, working on the *Cable Venture* refit, I went home and began planning my long-term future. Regular worldwide contracts at sea had served my degree objectives very well. Moving on aged 42, I needed to secure a long-term future in permanent employment and put my recent degree and project skills to good use. I therefore approached my job search with an open mind, turning down an early offer as Second Mate in UK coastal ships. Smart worldwide cable ships had raised my aspiration levels; however, no longer youthful, full-time sea-service with a first-rate global shipowner was an ideal but unlikely prospect. A full-time post at sea with Trinity House would have been a perfect, but unlikely event. Overall, good prospects at sea appeared limited in 1988. Even a possible door with Cable and Wireless did not open. I also needed to use my newly obtained BA (Hons) degree if possible. Therefore, I began to consider focusing my skills in the totally new world of Further Education (FE). An opportunity soon appeared on my radar. In time, this new area of work would open up a challenging world of sea-service as a deck officer in the UK fleet of ocean-going sail training ships.

In August 1988, I was short-listed to attend an interview for a position as a staff lecturer at the newly formed North East Worcestershire College, with a campus close to my home. The post was advertised as a position delivering core units to students following BTEC business programmes; all very new to me, therefore I attended an interview more in hope than in serious anticipation of success (I needed experience of interviews for academic posts). However, I had attended a college 'fireside chat' to discuss this new opportunity prior to making my application; and in so doing, I established a rapport with college managers. In all honesty, the more I learned about the specifics of the job, the less appealing it became; but it presented a real graduate challenge. I was interviewed on the day by a large panel including the newly appointed Principal and various senior members of staff. I presented a clear summary of my recent role as Deck Officer, serving with Trinity House Channel Cable, all delivered with appropriate gravitas. It seemed to do the trick, and I walked out of the interview with the offer of a permanent job and an incremental salary. The job would involve teaching aspects of BTEC Finance and Business units, including a BTEC subject entitled

People in Organisations; delivered mainly to young students with business aspirations. (I would need to read a few books on the subject of 'finance'). There were many students enrolled at the college with travel in mind; it was suggested that because I was a globally travelled man, this would go down well with certain aspiring young business students. What was I taking on? A mixed rattle bag saga of the world of UK Further Education was about to unfold. I would need quick thinking on my feet. I would need my seaman's survival skills and stamina.

I found many good-hearted staff at NEW College; but I was soon to discover the real reason for my appointment. My role was to wade through the murky waters of a pocket of alleged unrest, all unfortunately linked to a hearsay history of poor staff supervision in some sections of FE work on campus. The first year would therefore become another baptism of fire. The impression had formed in my head that places of learning were all similar to my past experience of nautical college and recent higher education. All college supervisors and academic staff were, without exception, persons of sound purpose? In an ideal world perhaps. On the positive side, the college was open to fresh ideas. There would also be some early consolation for me as a seaman: after starting my lecturing career in September 1988, I was soon also managing adult night classes: teaching Royal Yachting Association navigation courses to motivated part-time 'night-school' adults, including local GPs, business people, marine engineers and at least one NHS Consultant. This was very satisfying work; the NEW College managers also agreed that I could begin voyages in UK Sail Training ships as a kind of regular 'real world' work placement (staff were encouraged to follow such links as part of ongoing professional development). Sail training and sea-duty would become my eventual refuge, as the following pages will testify. However, there would be some testing FE college moments to recall. An unusual focus for my degree.

One of my earliest recollections from my initial lecturing challenge at NEW College concerns an overseas visit soon after my appointment, with a group of full-time teenage students. I say overseas – which is really a minor exaggeration. I was instructed by senior staff to arrange a grand tour of Paris for some leading academic staff, who would then use their combined wisdom and language skills to introduce my large party of students to the cultural delights of the French capital. We would stay in a budget Paris Youth Hotel and take in the sights and sounds of the city. All to be accomplished during a five-day coach tour from the UK. In theory at least, I would lead the Parisian party.

The Youth Hotel was very good value: it was located in central Paris overlooking Notre Dame Cathedral, and was clean and comfortable. Apart from the usual central pickpocket encounter in an unguarded student moment, followed by a prolonged statement-making visit to a local police post, everything worked like clockwork. Until the day of a planned voyage on the Seine. We were all to be embarked on the world famous Bâteaux-Mouches (Seine River Boats). Like most close encounters with threats of a violent outcome, the following boatman incident had a simple misunderstanding at its centre.

On riverside arrival there was an argument between a fluent French speaking colleague and the riverboat Ticket Office just before embarkation. Something to do with our group discount. Our man had excellent language skills, but failed the European diplomacy test. Riverboat security staff were soon involved in the developing altercation. However, national pride was now at stake; and war was declared as our middle-aged academic vaulted over the turnstile to face much French anger. From a distance I witnessed it all, and decided that our man squaring up to French security in the form of a shaven head, weight-lifter neck and towering stature was not a clever move. So I put my own verbal skills to good use – protesting with calm assurance that I was a reasonable man. We would sort this out. The riverboat security officer demonstrated that he had the measure of the invader. The relaxed shaven-headed officer turned to me and declared that whereas I might be a reasonable man, my turnstile-jumping Lone Ranger was not. On that day, a French security guard summed up his own view of British Further Education using unprintable language. More the vulgar boatman than Volga Boatman. Nevertheless, war was over; and the officials allowed us to embark on our insane-Seine cruise without further argument over discount. I confess that after the incident I had some serious doubts about several observed facets of FE college life. Later on, back at the UK base, I was called out on one occasion to the office of the same academic, having been informed that a student was about to jump out of the office window. As the office was located on the ground floor, I knew that all the alarm bells were of no account. No harm done. The bizarre world of my early turbulent daily life in UK Further Education. Give me a ship.

Within two years I was looking for a worthwhile 'in-house' project to try to make some sense of the general FE college culture. After initial lecturing, I was seeking, in my mid-forties, a manageable anchor for the sake of my own peace of mind. The project that I was about to grasp with both hands would eventually lead me back to sea. In 1991, I was in the right place at the right time in life, even if it was an uphill climb. I quickly learned the art of dealing with ridiculous and ambiguous situations as we approached the end of the decade. Never to lose one's sense of the ridiculous became my own middle-aged mantra. A footnote to these comments: one very positive skill came out of my early finance classes: I taught myself to construct cashflow charts and passed this on to my students. Therefore, when applying for a substantial new house mortgage, I used the same cashflow skills as I approached a local building society for the new loan. They took one look at my detailed cashflow chart and gave me a decision on the spot – to lend me 100% of my request. Further education paid out staff dividends.

Back to my personal further education rescue project; destined to become my main FE legacy. My project was built on my seafaring experience and my Kurt Hahn inspired degree studies. It all began in 1991. My concept involved training students for Uniformed and Emergency Services – aimed at school-leavers looking to the future. I was initially told by NEW College managers to forget the whole idea. However, I persisted with my educational concept, based on the North Country dictum that 'shy bairns get nowt'. After the initial launch, growth was remarkable: several West Mercia police officers, up to the rank of District Superintendent, would be very prominent in the early ongoing development of my new courses. Support would also come, as my courses became established, from the high ranks of both ACPO, HMIC and UK Armed Services. I was personally encouraged and also indebted to such high levels of support and genuine interest. Our rapid expansion of these challenging programmes, based on experiential learning including sail training and winter mountain expeditions, thrived on the back of the professional support of serving officers. As a result, my career at NEW College began to take off; but always with the help and encouragement outlined above.

In summary: we launched a hybrid Uniformed Services course with twelve students in 1991. Within two years we had grown to an intake of eighty full-time students. In addition to the student intakes, momentum was also established by recruiting a team of lecturing staff with police and armed services seniority; this included welcoming a newly retired PTI from the Royal Navy. I was privileged to lead and develop this solid and professional lecturing team with a common purpose. Our students thrived on the smart dress code, outdoor pursuits and an ongoing health and fitness programme, plus regular expeditions at Outdoor Centres and on local rivers. A symbiosis: students thrived; my career took off thanks to a focus on excellence.

Our jewel in the crown was to be the eventual development of a higher education course in the mid-1990s: HND Leadership Studies. Probably before its time, this full-time course was a genuine 'first' and was developed in primary partnership with West Mercia Constabulary – with the Army and Royal Marines taking a keen interest in the background. In common with any worthwhile project, there was a real cost involved; I gained official approval to run the programme by writing up the course from scratch; but this involved burning the midnight oil alongside my college management and lecturing duties. However, the resulting validation and recruitment of students was well worth the effort. In addition to gaining credit for higher education academic units, my students also served as Special Constables within local police shifts, working in close deployment with regular Friday night police operations. Students were assessed as they gained operational experience – and this success resulted in further academic units towards their final HND qualification. My role as Course Manager also expanded as I joined the same operational police shifts on a regular basis (with senior police backing): I was privileged to work regular police shifts alongside the same rapid response uniformed teams on patrol, over several years. By

Crew working far above the ocean.

personally turning up at serious crime or road traffic incidents in a response vehicle, as part of the police team on a busy night shift, or on New Year's Eve shifts – I gained a lot of 'street cred' from both regular officers and my patrolling students. This also fed into my time with students during my regular lectures, fitness training in the local pool, winter mountain training in North Wales and on sail training voyages. Kurt Hahn would smile at the experiential learning models employed. After two years on our HND Leadership programme and Special Constable Police shifts, many students gained old heads on young shoulders and were ready for the world of Emergency Services. My HND courses were a cross between old style police cadet training and adventures at sea, with winter mountains and rivers included for good measure.

I had been fortunate during my employment at NEW College, to start sail training voyages in early 1989 with the backing of senior FE managers. It all began as a voyage in a voluntary officer role, deployed as Watch Officer serving in the sail training ship (STS) *Malcolm Miller*. My first voyage opened a new chapter, under the command of Captain Adrian Allenby RN (Rtd). We got on well from that first voyage. I joined the ship on one dark and stormy night in Southampton; the *Malcolm Miller* was moored alongside the Sea Cadet vessel STS *Royalist*. The *Miller's* senior officer team on joining my first sail training ship was formidable: Captain Allenby (RN) plus a Merchant Navy Mate with a

Master's Certificate – Bob Stephenson. They both made me very welcome. They were experienced, down to earth seamen; and in the years between 1989 and 2000, it was my pleasure to spend many weeks at sea in their schooner company. I was destined to complete several voyages with Captain Allenby in Sail Training Association (STA) vessels: STS *Sir Winston Churchill* and STS *Malcolm Miller*. Adrian Allenby would eventually sadly leave the STA; Bob Stephenson would go on to become a Senior Master of square-rigged sailing vessels, fully rigged as brigs to replace the aging schooners. Without exception, I also got on well with both seamen during those early schooner and later brig voyages.

Seafarers form a strong bond when working in demanding ships and sail training would always be demanding for one reason or another from 1989 onwards. I would go on to sail in the new brigs STS *Prince William* and STS *Stavros S. Niarchos* as a Navigating Officer, on a salaried basis. But between my first voyage under sail in 1989 and my first voyage as a brig deck officer, there was much more work to be done. While I was employed in my normal role as course leader at NEW College, my regular voyages to sea became a refreshing counter to the constant college funding pressures. Regular restructuring occurred in FE. During almost twelve years on the staff at my own college, we endured many unsettling rearranging of deck chairs. But I was permitted room to explore my own local police partnership and continue my new seagoing adventures; and eventually several groups of Uniformed and Emergency Service students would start making regular sea voyages in sail training ships. Overall, we established at NEW College a whole group of new courses: all included demanding Welsh mountain residentials as part of our course development.

It was a lively time between 1988 and 2000. Some students ventured as far as the Canary Islands, embarked in the schooner STS *Sir Winston Churchill*. Alongside my ongoing work in close and regular contact with West Mercia police officers, regular sea voyages made for a very satisfying life. In addition, for me as course leader, winter mountain challenges with my students made the whole business of further education a very worthwhile project – far beyond my early introduction to college life. Parents praised the opportunities my team had opened up for students; and over the years students came back with thanks for our work. Students finished their courses with demanding challenges before moving into the world of work.

Students learned from real teamwork tests during their wild mountain days. We established an annual Ten Peaks Challenge in the rugged hills and valleys of Snowdonia, which developed to include an overnight in the wild winter weather. On one memorable occasion in 1999, we mountain-walked in driving rain with full kit for five hours 'on the hill', over challenging terrain and eventually found our overnight bothy. Twenty rain-soaked, tired and cold students and staff piled into stone accommodation space made for ten adults. The mood was very low with nobody speaking. But a transformation took place – something impossible to learn from the internet. We lit the pot-bellied stove and prepared hot drinks and hot food for everyone. Food over, we then set up an impromptu late concert. Everyone in the party was suddenly laughing and smiling, while outside the winter weather raged on. Team bonding. A lesson in teamwork and leadership indeed. Experiential learning. Overnight, I slept on the mess table in the bothy. We rose to a fresh day and then completed our Ten Peak Challenge, leaving our students to recount their own tales of derring-do.

Once again, I look back on that time in life with great affection. My students were always fit and happy. Between us we established something of a legend at NEW College. I was again in the right place at the right time, leading a team of very experienced former armed service officers and well-motivated young people. Eventually my military team gained all the experience they needed to run the show. I have accepted in life that there is always a time to move on. Nobody should hang on forever. By the year 2000, I was ready for a new challenge.

I found the right mind-set in terms of aspiration. It was all about sail training in the long haul – as I approached the new millennium and my 55th birthday loomed. But the specialised world of sail training ships as an employment opportunity? And how? There were practical problems to address. How does anyone return to seafaring aged 55? In addition to several practical problems, new technology at sea favoured the computer literate, a hurdle for me with only basic IT skills. Regular revalidation of UK seafaring qualifications was also required, plus the legally required strict medicals every two years for someone of my age. Returning to sea required an honest appraisal, even with sail training vessels in mind: it was a very limited option; therefore, it would take a bold move and still leave me open to failure. However, during my Uniformed and Emergency Services programmes of study, I had served as the course PTI when required. Aged 55, I was still fit and active. I was prepared to face the challenge of the harsh environment at sea, on a full-time basis if required. An opportunity presented itself as I prepared for a late-life ocean challenge. Back to the vision of an albatross battling the southern seas. My voyage ahead would include some stormy seas; it would also provide a pathway to employment into my 70th year. I would move on from Welsh mountains to climbing ships' masts.

Chapter 14

Stormy Seas – The gull's way and the whale's way

Sail training and yachting are different concepts. UK bookshops are full of yachting voyages, some by prominent authors; some by extraordinary British Knights of the Realm: Francis Chichester was an aviator; Chay Blyth a former para; Robin Knox-Johnston a former Merchant Navy officer. Some yachting adventures are remarkable. I recall talking to a lone Austrian yachtsman ashore in the Azores: he had sailed single-handed from Guadalupe. He spoke of sailing solo to the Antarctic. However, Tall Ships are different. Something stirring and primitive about a sail-training crew capturing a fair wind to drive their vessel through the hours of darkness. I began this Tall Ships' adventure in the older STA schooners in 1989; and would later serve in square-rigged vessels until 2015. Square-rigged sailing ships can be slow, and difficult to handle at times. Sail training is all about crews working-up their ship: and especially about a voyage crew of voluntary sailors who get on and complete the hard grind: such is the stuff of sea shanty and modern Tall Ship voyages. It is the romance of the sea etched on the faces of a very close circle of young men and women, doing what needs to be done. All hands aloft. Masefield captured the hard knocks of endless toil in *The Crowd*. The English poet reflected on pay-off day as the crew finally left their docked sailing ship… as captured in this extract of Tall Ships' verse.

After long months of water and the sky
These twenty saw the prison doors unlock.
These twenty men were free to quit the ship,
To tread dry land and slumber where they chose,
To count no bells that counted their repose,
To waken free from python Duty's grip.
What they had suffered and had greatly been
Was stamped upon their faces; they were still
Haggard with the indomitable will
That singleness of purpose had made clean.
John Masefield

Joseph Conrad was more philosophical: 'The ship, our ship, the ship we serve, is the moral symbol of our lives'. A long-forgotten literary critic once wrote, 'Conrad is trying to tell us something very important about the sea; about life'.

My New Millennium journey into salaried employment in the world of sail training began in Arctic seas. I gained regular OOW sea-time by joining UK Royal Fleet Auxiliary vessels in 2000/01. I say regular; but RFA *Sir Tristram* in the Arctic in 2001, on occasion joining HMS *Invincible* during fjord exercises, was anything but regular. Arctic sea-service aged 55 years was for me a significant move, involving sea time plus further nautical science courses, to provide an expanded range of qualifications. The RFA presented me with this open door in November 2000, with an offer of appointment at sea as Third Officer, until age 60 if I wanted it. I signed on and completed my first commission by joining RFA *Sir Tristram* for my series of winter Arctic voyages, ending in March 2001. I was surprised by the warm welcome. This genuine RFA officer bonding continued throughout, as we ventured north into the Norwegian Arctic and the regular winter base in Harstad (68°48'N) – moored in the centre of town next to the local Hogskolen (Uni College). While we loaded Arctic equipment in Marchwood, I briefed a Special Forces exercise. In Norway it was planning, waiting and then exercising in close quarters with RN and allied ships. I served in two RFA ships including one of the complex 'Fort' ships – RFA *Fort Rosalie*. My two RFA sea appraisals confirmed me as a safe OOW. RFA service was very encouraging for a seaman of 55 years, albeit lacking computer skills. However, my wife and I concluded that the normal RFA four-month tours at sea were too long at our stage in life. Therefore, I went ashore in September 2001, having gained extra worthwhile sea-time as OOW. *Conclusion:* the RFA remains an excellent organisation. My whole Arctic experience, in company with the Royal Navy, raised my skills profile and gave me extra confidence to serve in Tall Ships. My mantra from Arctic service was to treat everything as a training exercise. Bonus: I gained my UK MCA Chief Mate certification from my sea service with the RFA.

After gaining challenging OOW experience during 2000–2001, I also preserved 'irons in the fire' work ashore when necessary to continue paying the mortgage if seafaring stalled for any reason; so, I did whatever was required at sea or ashore to keep income flowing into our bank account, while preserving my main interest and links with sail training and the sea in general. I did further work for some local FE colleges (which I found less to my liking after the freedom enjoyed during my long Uniformed and Emergency Services sojourn at NEW College). However, sail training remained my long-term focus throughout. Apart from a short taster voyage in the new STA brigs in 2000, my total experience of sail training ships up to 2001 had been in the STA schooners. My schooner voyages as Watch Officer had been extensive during my tenure at NEW College from 1989 onwards – in UK coastal waters as far north as the Orkney Islands, close European ports, Norway, Baltic ports and the Canary Islands. However, with the advent of the larger and more complex STA brigs, I needed to maintain sea-time if I was to make serious inroads as a regular Tall Ships' officer. So, my next major step in navigating the new brigs was to fly to the Swedish Port of Gothenburg in spring 2002, and from there, begin intensive training as a seaman/Officer of the Watch in square rigged sailing ships. A major step – resulting in a UK Northern Marine certificate declaring my competence to serve as OOW in Tall Ships – part of Northern Marine's overall ship management of training brigs. These vessels would become my clear focus until 2015. (I would serve in seven UK Tall Ships).

I also gained challenging sea-time as OOW by flying out to Darwin, Northern Australia in early 2003, when a UK cruise ship manager needed an experienced deck officer at short notice, to join his 'Flag of Convenience' vessel. He gave me ample warning of the task: to survive my 12 weeks in the tense atmosphere of his ship. There would be two phases to the deployment: Phase One – Six weeks Darwin to UK; Phase Two – Six weeks of short sea voyages. The reality for me: a shakedown deep-sea voyage, followed by a phase operating beyond my comfort zone. So, I embarked in Darwin to serve as OOW (solo 8–12 Deck Officer), in a grand old ship we will call *Mercator*, responsible for the safe navigation of the ship during my watch, with hundreds of passengers embarked.

For the first time in my experience, I would receive orders to alter course to avoid rain-clouds ahead. We sailed to Singapore, then crossed the Indian Ocean to Durban and Cape Town, then on into the Atlantic calling at St Helena, Dakar and Lisbon; we then arrived safe and sound in the UK. I survived the hard-working voyage from Darwin with no incidents. On UK arrival, I attended a long debrief with the Staff Captain. His supportive comments were welcome after the endless duty. I had six weeks still to endure until my relief arrived. My wife Elaine joined me for the final 14-night Med-cruise: an unusual but very welcome bonus. All very encouraging. However, the onboard 'mood music' seemed to change during my final weeks of service; and I forced myself to recognise that my age, as I approached 60, was perhaps not my strongest point during those final high-octane sea days. However, I completed my twelve-week deployment unscathed, with warm hearted best wishes from fellow crew members as I disembarked.

When it was all over, I remained content to continue with my UK Tall Ship duties. My voyage halfway around the world had been remarkable, with 800 souls embarked. My professional sea duties had been observed by fellow deck officers who were always helpful and supportive. My own sea-history (regular onboard assessments as OOW) often rated me 'above average', (sometimes 'excellent'). Therefore my 'satisfactory' OOW record from the cruise ship was acceptable to me – given the several personal challenges faced during the deployment. No accidents. My seafaring strengths were well described in a later general job reference. For me, it was an illuminating OOW interlude. *My conclusion:* no wish for another cruise-ship deployment any time soon. But it was good experience.

The Marine Superintendent had earlier flagged a warning. He sent me on a fully funded end-of-contract college course (supported by a staff car and expenses, plus his first-class work reference). I had been available to serve at short notice in early 2003, when the 'Super' faced his unforeseen manning crisis: but I faced an unusual deployment in his ship – which I managed to survive. On reflection, the Australia to UK voyage proved that my age was in fact no barrier to ongoing sea-service, providing I maintained professional certification. But, approaching 60 years of age, I concluded that I was unlikely to obtain full-time employment at sea, even in sail training ships.

My blunt summary: time for a rethink. Perhaps I could continue part-time as an officer in UK Tall Ships? And that is where my future would be worked out to the age of 69 years. I simply adapted my plans to part-time service: this pragmatic approach worked. My own record of regular life-time seafaring was destined to remain accident free. Calm waters ahead.

Following my Australia – UK OOW experience, I began to make further OOW voyages in the new STA brigs. My other need for a secure salaried position was satisfied in late 2003 within the graduate sector ashore. The key added bonus: this new appointment began with sufficient seniority to provide a living salary, but also gave me maximum paid leave to continue my part-time Tall Ships' career. I would be able to cover our living costs, and also follow my seafaring ambitions. My new shore-based employer was to be the local NHS (PCT), who required an experienced problem solver/graduate to build a close partnership across the public sector, and deliver key public health messages to the local county population. I would be working on these issues with senior Fire officers, Environmental Health officers and public servants in related fields. We would set up a working alliance. Tobacco issues was making national headlines; and there was much work to be done raising awareness in the population. A far cry from seafaring, but I had recent transferable skills to employ. Education was a prime area of operations; I would find myself working with Worcester Warriors Rugby Squad visiting local high schools to raise fitness and smoking issues. Together we invented and delivered, 'Walk the Warrior Way on Smoking'. I would go on to deliver the presentation, fully booted and spurred in Warriors' Rugby kit, to 80% of the high schools in Worcestershire. We also went on to develop from scratch 'Heart Smart Homes': Fire Safe – Active – Smokefree. This was rolled out via the local Sure Start centres.

In the meanwhile, I needed to also continue to 'Walk the Sailor Way' on the decks of Tall Ships. In 2004/05, I completed a few voyages, as required, to reinforce my Tall Ship seaman officer skills; however, my 'take-off moment' came in 2006 when my local NHS employer invited anyone interested to apply for unpaid extra leave. I took up the offer and flew to Italy to join STS *Stavros S. Niarchos* at sea. This would become a major step forward; I joined the ship as salaried permanent crew for a voyage across the Mediterranean. Again: right place – right time. Is that an enduring ocean-going albatross on my sea horizon? The grace of God; the ongoing kindness of strangers in a difficult world. I was 60 plus, and holding down two contrasting fields of professional work. I was able to pass strict seamanship medicals and revalidate my MCA professional certificate as Chief Mate every five years. A charmed life, if ever there was such a thing; and a greatly blessed grandparent also. Life was as good as it gets: robust sea service and grandchildren's games. I have lifelong memories of our grandchildren at play. Also, lifelong memories of my Tall Ship voyages.

The schooners themselves played a major role in UK sail training. They were generally run like a public school at sea. The young voyage crew members were billeted below the Main-Deck, in the Half-Deck with bunk space for 42 sailors. Ship's officers lived and worked amidships, with the panelled Chartroom as the operational centre of the ship. My early role as one of three Watch Officers was to take charge of the Open Bridge when the schooner was at sea, with an on-watch team including helm and lookouts. There were three watches of 13, plus a Watch Leader (WL). Watches were named after the vessels three masts: Fore Watch; Main Watch; Mizzen Watch. Each day, two crew members from each Watch would serve as 'Dayworkers' and 'Galley Rats'. It was well organised and highly enjoyable. The Chartroom was a sea-sanctuary, with the Captain's cabin close by. Officers dined together in the Chartroom. It was close-quarters living within a well organised routine, underpinned by demanding seamanship. I thrived in this onboard environment. I experienced no bad voyages in a schooner, and was sad to witness their eventual demise approaching the year 2000. The *Churchill* and the *Miller* were special ships, offering unique seagoing memories. Larger STA brigs had similar routines; but never quite matched the schooners for onboard atmosphere. However, we are all called to move on. It was a great time in the history of modern Tall Ships. Great to have been there.

Malcolm Miller: French Coast.
Jo Gauthier.

Royal guest and Sir Winston
Churchill's crew.

Sir Winston Churchill's port lookout.

Sir Winston Churchill: bowsprit.

I remain indebted to my sea-service from age 16 in large ocean-going ships. However, such service places global seafarers sometimes at a distance from the extreme nature of the wind and the sea. By contrast, my 25 years of sail training experience was a unique way to rediscover both the savage elements and the romance of the sea. Also, it is interesting to contrast and compare the elegant lines of the two STA Schooners with the two bulky square-rigged STA brigs, commissioned to replace the schooners as the year 2000 dawned.

As I look back on my seafaring days, it was my privilege to be a part of my many distant voyages in merchant ships; and later in life, in both classes of sail training ships. To begin my Tall Ships' experience as a volunteer Watch Officer, serving in the schooners from 1989 – and eventually to end my seafaring days in 2015, as salaried permanent crew in square-rigged ships is recalled as a great honour. In globally deployed ships of the Merchant Navy, I slowly learned my early skills as a seafarer; but during my Arctic-serving RFA voyages, and at sea in sail training schooners and modern brigs, I developed the skills and attitudes of a hands-on seaman officer. There is a difference. And to be employed at sea into my 70th year in any of my ocean-going Tall Ships was also richly rewarding. I served in seven UK Tall Ships; and was always invited back for more sea-service over my 25-year involvement. The memory fills me with a deep sense of accomplishment even as I sit and write in 2022. I recall the words of Joseph Conrad, as one of his fictitious characters (in the renamed *Children of the Sea*, 1897) looked back and recalled long-lost shipmates:

> *The dark knot of seaman drifted in the London sunshine… to the right of the group the stained front of The Mint, cleansed by a flood of light. The crew drifted out of sight. I never saw them again. The sea took some; the steamers took others; the graveyards of the earth will account for the rest… Good-bye shipmates. You were a good crowd. As good a crowd as ever fisted with wild cries, the beating canvas of a heavy foresail; or working aloft, invisible in the night, gave back yell for yell to a westerly gale.*

The ability of the crew of a sailing ship to work together and, in harmony, facing difficulty as a supportive team, draws great affection from Conrad. There is not only intrinsic moral value in such activity at the time, but also in its later recollection. In today's high-tech computer driven world of work – such writing sums up the richness of my own sail-training experience. I was part of the modern Tall Ships' world for 25 years, sometimes as volunteer crew; sometimes as salaried, permanent crew. But either way, I was richly rewarded – beyond measure.

My own late sea-memories are based on the unique challenge of my Tall Ships years; on the unique character of the individual ships; and on the individual chemistry of the crews. On the storms; on the calms; on the howling wind; on the sea state; on North Sea crossings against head-winds; on halcyon days of voyaging to the UK from the mid-Atlantic Azores. Some days resembled cut diamonds; other days were just heavy going. It is with this recent experience in mind that I shall close this account of my adventures. So, what was it like to seek to master the skills required in order to simply survive a sea voyage in a modern sail training ship, even as an experienced global mariner? I would suggest that it begins with mastering the unique terminology employed. This is more than simply referring to a deck, or to port and starboard. There exists a whole new vocabulary to learn and work with. Any class of ship can attract a baffling array of technical language; but before we get into any depth, it is best not to be too technical. For example, a navigator might refer, not to a clock, but to a marine chronometer, and possibly refer to the development of the early marine time-keepers developed by Harrison et al. However, if you read, with a sharp eye, the accounts of the solo round-the-world voyages of the American Master Mariner Joshua Slocum, you will discover that he used an old kitchen clock to aid his calculation of longitude at sea. So much for technical innovation. I still value the celestial spheres, haversines and Norrie's Tables of my cadet officer days at sea.

Returning to voyage preparation and terminology. The managers of UK Tall Ships from the late 1980s, in my experience, always sent out joining instructions, often accompanied by advice on crew safeguarding on one hand, and technical information on the other. Therefore, I will begin with my first voyage as Watch Officer in STS *Malcolm Miller* in 1989. My early Watch Officer's brief began:

> *There are no other vessels in the world with quite the same aims as the STA schooners. As a prospective Watch Officer, you will be a sailor with sound seamanship knowledge and detailed experience of UK coastal waters. But our ship's gear is heavy; the reaction is slow but relentless once an action at sea is started.*

This was good preparation. The brief continues…

> *At sea, the Watch Officer on duty is responsible for keeping a proper lookout, all sail trimming, the use of preventers, all helm orders and courses steered; and you will give all executive orders to the Duty Watch. You are expected to take bearings of approaching targets (other ships) to ascertain risk of collision.*

It was a demanding (never really off-duty) role, working in partnership with the Duty OOW. The Duty Watch Officer kept watch on the open bridge for 4 hours at a time, and carried responsibility for the effective command of the vessel under sail at sea, (unless the Captain, another permanent deck officer or pilot 'had the con'). In addition, you were expected to manage the Watch of 13 young people through their appointed youthful Watch Leader. I learned to manage the role of Watch Officer by forming a partnership with the Watch Leader. It was simple: as Watch Officer I would back-up the Watch Leader during all sail handling on deck or aloft; I would then expect the WL to support me in every operation on the open bridge: in particular, the role of the lookouts and the role of maintaining any given course to steer. In my experience, the partnership never failed. For every member of the watch, it was excellent teamwork and leadership training. And then there was the terminology of the world-famous Three Masted Topsail Schooners, *Sir Winston Churchill* and *Malcolm Miller*. As sail training ships they were almost identical sisters. The vast terminology applied equally to both vessels. And, there is always the humorous side to any ship at sea. Not many seafarers understand the term 'Baggywrinkle'. Not in any dictionary. But it is a kind of knitted yarn attached to the standing rigging of a sailing ship – to prevent the sails chaffing when deployed. So 'Baggywrinkle' prevents wear and tear of the ship's sails. (Not making this up). I eventually found a reference in *The Pocket Oxford Guide to Sailing Terms*, Dear and Kemp, Oxford University Press, 1987. This seafaring kit is also known as 'Bag-o'-Wrinkle'.

Sailing ship terms represent a whole world of trade and discovery by sea; they also represent the daily shipboard life of past generations of (mainly) young men who ventured out, away from city squalor or from the hamlet, the forest or the plough: the lot of 'Mercantile Jack' sailing before the mast. Therefore, sail training today, seeks to rediscover the joys of the demanding seafaring life, without the months of servitude endured by past generations. An ABC of terms will suffice to outline the alien world of sailing ship life, given to officers before joining any sail training ship. In addition, *Eagle Seamanship* (a US Coastguard training handbook published by the US Naval Institute, Annapolis) is essential reading for any new officer serving in any sail training vessel across the globe.

Athwartships: At right angle to the fore and aft line of the ship.
Braces: Running rigging (as opposed to Standing Rigging): hauled away during manoeuvres, e.g. to tack and wear the ship. (Order 'Stand-by for Bracing Stations.'), n.b. All rigging and sails maintained by the Boatswain (Bosun).
Chief Mate: Deck Officer (2nd in Command). Executive Officer: responsible for running a civilian sailing ship according to the lawful orders of the Master.
Downhaul: Any line that pulls down a sail during sail handling (see Halyard).
ER: The Engine Room (n.b. Chief Engineer province on sailing vessels).
Footropes: To aid working aloft, and running under yardarms – steel-wire ropes rigged for the booted feet of crew working on the yards.
Gasket: Line or strap used to secure a square sail when furled.
Halyard: Line used for setting sails. (Haul away Joe).
In-its-gear: When a square sail is held tight up to its yard.
Jackstay: Metal bar running along the top of a yard.
Knock-down: Term used to describe a sailing vessel laid over by a violent wind.
Leeward: The side of the ship opposite to the windward side.
MCA: UK Maritime Coastguard Agency.
Navigating Officer: Deck officer responsible for overall ship navigation.
OOW: Officer of the Watch (Duty OIC Bridge or Engine Room).
Preventer: A safety line rigged to prevent a boom from swinging.

Quick-Flash: Characteristic of the light of a navigation aid, e.g. a lit buoy.
Ratlines: Lines attached to the shrouds to act as rungs for climbing aloft.
Stopper: A short length of rope used in mooring-line operations.
Tack: Pass the bow of a sailing ship through the wind. (See Wear Ship below).
Unfurl: To cast loose a square sail by throwing off the gaskets.
Vang: A line controlling the end of a gaff.
Wear Ship: Change tack by taking the Tall Ship's stern through the wind.
X: Part of the PZX spherical triangle used in celestial navigation at sea.
Yardarm: The outer end of a vessel's yard (e.g. port yardarm).
Zenith: That point in the heavens being directly overhead the observer.

Despite essential training alongside, before proceeding to sea, the hazards of sail training are very real from embarkation onwards. Despite expert supervision and attention to training detail, accidents happen at sea. Without serious injury to any crew member involved (including the fall from aloft), I witnessed the following accident during a schooner voyage some years ago. It occurred on a calm, sunny morning – during our routine departure from an Irish seaport.

The STS *Malcolm Miller* was leaving her Dún Laoghaire berth after a short visit. All crew were at harbour stations: with 'hands aloft' on the largely decorative fore mast yards (voyage crew on the lower yard including my own senior college students). The ship was low in the water compared to the level of the quay's hard-standing surface; our rib was in the water ready to recover our line-party ashore as we departed. Slowly our ship let-go and inched forward TMO (To Master's Orders). We were also heaving-away to recover our starboard anchor. It was a slow departure from our berth. The accident happened in slow motion, as in a dream. It could have been a fatal disaster. It was a very close call indeed.

No crew member on departure had observed that the shore-facing brace (of the lower portside yardarm) had snagged on the quayside. The brace was secured to a steel wire rope (attached to the schooner's manned lower yard) by means of a simple block-and-tackle rig. As the ship inched forward, the easy tension on the lower port yardarm slowly became massive tension, due to the snagged line – and the 'purchase' effect of the block and tackle. (The opposite starboard brace was secured tight). The port-side tension mounted until the lower (massive) wooden yard exploded at its centre with a loud canon-fire crack. The six young sailors on the lower yard were all violently shaken off and left stranded and swinging – as their safety harnesses and tethers broke their fall to the deck. And certain injury. All except one. (Whenever I recall this event, I can still see a young female in flight 12 metres above the water of the dock – her flight-path of rapid descent just clear of the concrete jetty.) She was a very fortunate young casualty. Life-changing injury or worse was avoided on that bright Irish morning.

I was stationed on the fore deck and witnessed the catastrophic failure of the lower yard and the immediate distress situation, shouting out the timeless cry, 'Man Overboard'. The drama was over in seconds, but the rescue of our five young sailors aloft took some time. We all had two concerns: the voyage crew member in the water; and the voyage crew members stranded aloft. The young casualty in the water was picked up in smart time, by the crew of our already deployed power-driven rib. The casualty was shaken but apparently uninjured (according to attending Irish emergency paramedics). The rescue of our remaining five crew members aloft took some time. Four had managed to haul their bodies back on to the badly fractured yard (itself supported by standing rigging). One rugby-large male casualty was still dangling above the decks, tethered by his safety harness to the fractured yard. A quick-thinking member of the permanent crew climbed aloft and initiated the lowering to deck level of one bulky young man. Remarkably the whole incident resulted in no serious injury to any of the six young members of the distressed crew. The female crew member rescued from the dockside had slipped out of her adjustable upper-body safety harness – from her departure position at the extreme end of the lower yard, and fell many metres into the harbour water. On the day, everything worked out in favour of the casualty. Our ship's young crew quickly recovered its composure, shook off the incident and sailed for Greenock where the inquiry began.

No loss of life; no serious injury; but, some important lessons: in the longer-term, the accident resulted in a redesign of the compulsory harness – always deployed when working above deck height. In terms of sail training and other adventure activities for young and old at sea, SOLAS (Safety of Life at Sea) remained paramount. There is no place for reckless behaviour at sea, nor bad planning. There is no place for any lack of supervision, nor deployment of poor equipment. The sea will pay back any casual approach.

The dawn of the New Millennium saw the *Churchill* and the *Miller* retire from STA sea-service and the arrival of the brigs: the aforementioned *Prince William* and *Stavros S. Niarchos*. Several experienced STA Watch Officers, including the writer, took up the challenge of sailing in square rig from the year 2000 onwards. These square-rigged voyages offered a fresh dimension to UK sail training. The new brigs were large ocean-going sailing vessels – packed with all the latest technology and safety systems. Their deep-sea challenge was real and a joy to embrace. These brigs would keep me at sea into my 70th year – in 2015.

Halcyon Days: Deep Seas and Tall Ships

The shoreline is a place for contemplation
With sculptured forms of seabirds on the wing;
Pebble-pounding waves; white toothed Atlantic rollers;
And cloudburst rays of sunlight through the mind.

An ocean's mood is etched with contradiction
With silver paths of starlight on its face;
Transformed to depths of highly charged destruction;
Sharp iceberg forms of wind-eroded grace.

The oceans' call drives stout-hearts to adventure.
Stow mooring lines; plot courses on the chart;
Breathe deep the salt-stained air, and feel the wind-throb;
So let fair winds and Tall Ships lift my heart.
Peter John Hill, 2021.

Epilogue Alpha

My Tall Ships – Schooners and Brigs 1989–2015

There follows a postscript to my Tall Ships days from 1989 to 2015. Some notable voyages, Tall Ship Captains and crews. And always the call of the deep ocean.

The brigs PW and SSN captured on a Race Day.

My earliest voyages to sea in Tall Ships began in 1989 as mentioned in earlier chapters. As ever, it was a case of being in the right place at the right moment and using that moment to maximum advantage. I had placed adventure voyages in UK Tall Ships at the heart of my 1987 honours dissertation. This led to my appointment to the academic staff of North East Worcestershire College in 1988. In March 1989, I joined the crew of STS *Malcolm Miller* for an Easter voyage with the backing of NEW College managers. This seafaring appointment fed directly into my role as Course Leader, eventually developing Uniformed and Emergency Service courses to higher education level. (A massive unforeseen bonus: early

NEW College manager support established the Tall Ships' route to my final sea-service ending 2015). The following is a full list of my voyages as a Watch Officer sailing in STA Schooners; these regular voyages to European ports combined enough sea time, along with teaching RYA navigation courses, to preserve my seagoing skills. This provided the springboard to further seafaring during my working life after the age of 55. My RFA Arctic service and further Tall Ships voyages from the year 2000 also provided a platform for my senior years.

Date	Sail Training Schooner	Voyage as Watch Officer	Distance/ max wind	Master/OIC Schooner Voyage
1989	*Malcolm Miller* Call-Sign… MYFU Built 1967	Southampton Alderney St Malo Fowey	424 nautical miles (nm) Force 6	Captain A. Allenby RN (Rtd)
1990	*Sir Winston Churchill* Call-Sign… GRZZ Built 1966	Zeebrugge Amsterdam Amble anchorage Scarborough – anchor overnight Port of Tyne	744 nm Force 8	Captain Josh Garner MN
1991	*Sir Winston Churchill*	Cork Belfast Stromness Aberdeen	845 nm Force 6	Captain A. Allenby RN (Rtd) Royal visitor – Belfast
1992	*Sir Winston Churchill*	Kiel Gothenburg Copenhagen Wismar Kiel Canal Newcastle on Tyne	1081 nm Force 8	Captain A. Allenby RN (Rtd)
1994	*Malcolm Miller*	St Malo Cobh St Peter Port	915 nm Force 6	Captain R. Stephenson MN

Date	Sail Training Schooner	Voyage as Watch Officer	Distance/ max wind	Master/OIC Schooner Voyage
1995	*Malcolm Miller*	Frederikshavn Scheveningen Amsterdam	545 nm Force 6	Captain J. Etheridge MN
1995	*Malcolm Miller*	Amsterdam Kleven/Norway Den Helder/Holland Boston (UK)	1043 nm Force 7	Captain M. Forwood MN
1996	*Sir Winston Churchill*	Canaries: Las Palmas La Palma Gomera Los Cristianos Las Palmas	492 nm Force 7	Captain H. O'Neill MN
1997	*Malcolm Miller*	Weymouth Dún Laoghaire/Éire Greenock	619 nm Force 7	Captain M. Kemmis-Betty RN (Rtd)
1998	*Sir Winston Churchill*	Canaries: Santa Cruz de Tenerife La Palma Gomera Los Cristianos Santa Cruz TF	450 nm Force 8	Captain J. Etheridge MN
1999	*Sir Winston Churchill*	Poole Antwerp Gt Yarmouth Shoreham	762 nm Force 6	Captain J. Etheridge MN
2000	*Sir Winston Churchill*	Santa Cruz de Tenerife La Palma Gomera Las Palmas Santa Cruz TF	420 nm Force 5	Captain J. Etheridge MN

STA Schooners inbound from the North Sea: STS Sir Winston Churchill leading STS Malcolm Miller into a fairway. Acrylic sketch by the author, 2019.
Each training ship carried a total of 812 square metres of sail; and each ship provided accommodation for 55 crew members. Note the jumbo-size Mizzen sail (aft).

From my own schooner experience, Watch Officers came via two routes: Scheme One involved steady progress whereby an experienced RN or MN officer sailed as voyage crew in their own youth, and eventually sailed in *Sir Winston Churchill* or *Malcolm Miller* as a Watch Officer. This route was also open to those applicants who had extensive experience sailing large yachts. As an experienced MN deck officer, I could see how yachting experience could lead to someone making a success of the Watch Officer role. Scheme Two was my route whereby, (as an experienced seaman but with no experience of schooners or yachts), the STA was prepared to provide the opportunity to succeed as a Watch Officer. In my case writing my honours degree dissertation based on sail training opened the door. Hard evidence showed that it worked for me: early on in my schooner experience I received two letters of encouragement from schooner Captains following demanding voyages with young crews. The letter quoted below is from Captain Adrian Allenby RN (rtd). Sent from *Sir Winston Churchill* following my service as Watch Officer (Voyage C465): Kiel to Newcastle August 1992. The letter is dated 30th August 1992; Captain Allenby and I sailed on several voyages forming a strong seamanship bond. Allenby RN was always strict but fair.

> *Dear Peter, May I say how much I enjoyed sailing with you on the last* Churchill *voyage. Thank you for all the assistance you gave, helping to make the voyage one of*

the best I have ever done. The ship seemed very flat yesterday morning after you had all disembarked. We have continued to be buffeted by strong winds; I have decided to delay sailing until Tuesday to enable any new foreign crew members to explore Newcastle-upon-Tyne. I hope we sail again someday – and in the meanwhile my best wishes. Adrian.

It would be my final voyage with my fellow seaman Captain Adrian Allenby RN. An earlier letter dated August 1990 from Captain Joshua Garner MN reads:

Dear Peter, I want to thank you for your help on the recent Churchill *voyage C420. Watch Officers are forever invaluable at sea; I can assure you that I very much appreciate the contribution made by you and your fellow Watch Officers. It is especially satisfying to have other seamen embarked; I do find a special bonus sailing with experienced 'men of the cloth'. It is a fond hope that we might again sail together. Josh.*

Note: It was to be my only voyage with Josh Garner – who was later appointed to command a Royal Dhow in one of the Gulf States. A Captain Garner ambition: Hand signals only on his royal vessel – no raised voices.

At the start of the above August 1990 voyage, we sailed into the aftermath of the annual Tall Ships' Race youth celebrations in the North Sea shipping area. Amsterdam was often in the thick of port events when any such race included North Sea sailing. Josh Garner prepared the following edited summary of the 1990 Tall Ship summer activity, including the real impact on the *Churchill* crew joining in Zeebrugge for voyage C420: Voyage to Newcastle via Amsterdam. Josh Garner reported:

Sir Winston Churchill *joining arrangements worked very well, except for heavy road traffic in Zeebrugge causing us a long delay between our North Sea Ferry and the* Churchill *– moored safely in harbour. However, we eventually embarked our voyage crew of young men who were more than normally enthusiastic and dynamic. Zeebrugge was still heavy-laden with a fleet of Tall Ships in the port. Our harbour training routine was soon completed and the voyage crew were all given shore leave to explore Brugge and Zeebrugge before departing for Amsterdam and a series of Tall Ship events.*

Before departure from Zeebrugge, STS *Sir Winston Churchill* had an opportunity to enter into the spirit of any Tall Ships' Race, by way of an inter-crew exchange programme. Therefore, Captain Josh Garner continued his C420 entertaining voyage summary,

At the instigation of Tall Ships' Race 1990 official Admiral Vallings, the opportunity arose in Zeebrugge to exchange twelve Churchill Voyage Crew with twelve young crew... from other national ships... for the sea passage to Amsterdam. Our exchange seafaring friends fitted in very well sailing as Churchill crew, relishing the British food and our ship's hot showers. We finally reached Amsterdam, with its full and imaginative programme of many events for the international Tall Ship crews. Amsterdam organisers made a huge effort and were well prepared for our crews; the port event was big, and our young crews enjoyed the Amsterdam experience; but as sailing day arrived our own Sir Winston Churchill crew was glad to leave Amsterdam astern and sail out into the grey northern sea beyond.

Light winds prevailed as we crossed the North Sea, and our crew of young lads were all 'shaking down' well within the watch system and general ship routines. They relished the starlit night duties on the open bridge, the bioluminescence and leaping porpoises. The lonely sea and a sky full of wonder. All the hallmarks of a sail training voyage. Day followed day at sea and soon we arrived off the North East coast of the UK, with a visit to Amble. Our Amble anchorage and runs ashore

Author qualified as UK MCA Chief Mate (sail training) OOW (Unrestricted). Sailed frequently as permanent crew: Deck Officer responsible for navigation.

Meanwhile ashore – My grandchildren: Elliot, Isaac and Maddison in 2012.
Will there be any UK sail training ships left for their generation to experience?
By the year 2015 UK sail training was becoming a very expensive operation.

were always enlivened by Freddie the bottlenose dolphin. Finally, two days of
North Sea sailing in Force 8 winds enlivened the voyage; a few hours anchored off
Scarborough and then into the River Tyne and a passage up river to Newcastle with
a TV crew embarked. A very good voyage. Captain Joshua Garner, 1990.

Brig Captains Bob and Barbara would both contribute to my early experience and
training as a deck officer in the new brigs. Making the transition from service as a
Watch Officer in the renowned STA schooners – to professional seaman in the five
square-rigged vessels I eventually sailed in, was on par with my hard-won honours
degree. An unforgettable experience. My crew training in the new STA brigs,
(operated by Tall Ships Youth Trust: TSYT), began in March 2000, with a five day
'shake-down' voyage from Weymouth in STS *Stavros S. Niarchos*, under the
command of Captain Barbara Campbell. Together with her sister ship STS *Prince
William*, the ships presented officers and crews with a new formidable seamanship
challenge. This TSYT challenge would, from 2001, take me to the mid-Atlantic

Captain Bob Stephenson MN served at sea as Master of STA Schooners and STA Brigs over many years. Captain Bob enjoyed a long and distinguished Tall Ships career. He had the ability to quietly deal with many varied and stressful situations at sea and ashore. In both his seamanship and his quiet dignity, he was an inspiring example to all who knew him. I sailed with Captain Bob on many voyages, including my first Tall Ship voyage in 1989, when he was serving as Malcolm Miller's Mate (Chief Officer). In 2001, the UK MCA awarded me my seafaring certification as Chief Mate. I learned my brig seamanship skills from many seafarers including Captain Bob Stephenson, Captain Liam Keating, Captain John Etheridge, Captain Darren Naggs, Captain Dave Bainbridge and our female Tall Ships' Master Mariner Captain Barbara Campbell.

Azores, to the volcanic Canary Islands, into the Western and Central Mediterranean Sea, and into the Baltic Sea, in addition to all parts of the British Isles. This wide-ranging sea challenge would form my regular learning curve through the years 2000 to 2015, reinforced by similar deck officer service in a further three UK registered square-rigged sail training ships, as follows:

STS *Lord Nelson* (Jubilee Sailing Trust)
STS *Tenacious* (Jubilee Sailing Trust)
STS *Pelican of London* (Private Trust)

*Schooner:
Heavy Weather
Acrylic sketch by
the author, 2020.*

My personal sail training summary: a total of seven UK sail training ships over a period of 25 years (1989–2015), including the renowned STA schooners.

Simple examination of the sail plan alone of STS *Stavros S. Niarchos* indicates the scale of the learning curve for any experienced seafarer, compared to the significant (but smaller) operational challenge posed by the retiring schooners *Sir Winston Churchill* and *Malcolm Miller*. When I arrived in Weymouth for my March 2000 shake-down voyage in *Stavros*, I saw the masts of the ship soaring above the dockside buildings of the port. I would soon be donning my safety

*Complex sail
plan! Hands aloft
for 10 square sails
in each brig.*

harness and climbing high for the regular sea-training 'up and over' harbour routine. After that I would be scaling the heights at sea – as far as the Royals – the highest yards. The schooners had two yards on the foremast, i.e. just two square-sails on each ship. By contrast, the new brigs each had a build of 10 yards (20

Girl-power aloft: Working the yards.

Blue water: But where are the lads?

Teamwork high above the blue Med.

Behold the manpower.

yard-arms) on two masts; each training brig could set a total of 10 square sails plus 8 fore and aft sails. Tasks aloft indicated by my voyage photographs.

However, as I write in 2022, both TSYT training brigs have been sold off. Because of the spiralling costs involved running and crewing such complex square-rigged vessels, UK sail training ships similar to STS *Stavros S. Niarchos* may never be seen again. It was an honour to be part of their short 21st Century UK maritime history. Unique moments; unique voyages; unique crews. To have also served in the two STA schooners was an added bonus. 25 years of life-changing adventure.

My Weymouth based voyage, as a crew member in 2000, led to many more years of sail training exploits in UK square-rigged vessels. Crews would be given sheets of information on square-rigged sailing terms, sail-handling procedures, watch management, tacking and wearing ship and so on. The task list was endless. I elected to be trained both as a crew member and a seaman officer (MCA Chief Mate). I managed to survive the learning curves of both seamanship roles, eventually sailing as Officer of the Watch and primary Navigating Officer, undergoing many voyages in STS *Stavros S. Niarchos* (my main appointment over the years); but I also served at sea in STS *Prince William*, STS *Lord Nelson*, STS *Tenacious* and STS *Pelican of London*. Over time, I sailed with a variety of youth, adult and disabled crews: some involved UK coastal voyages; some involved long sea and ocean voyages; some involved Tall Ship races and related events. All voyages required a high level of crew safety and safeguarding procedure. I was qualified with my UK MCA Certification – plus ENG1 medicals supporting my advancing years. I managed to fulfil the demanding roles involved, with all the practical demands of seamanship. This included navigating the ship through every night at sea (Midnight–0400hrs OOW). To have been called back for further service by every Tall Ship manager I worked for to the age of 69, was a very rewarding way to end my lifetime association with ships and the sea. It was always a great honour to have been there and done it.

Integrity, communication skills, practical ability, detailed knowledge, confident decision making, empathy in the face of human frailty – plus the ability to organise and work with humour, is the pathway to success in any leadership role. I will conclude my lifetime account by going back to my own training and professional voyages in square-rigged training ships. Professional square-rigged sea-training began in 2000 and ended in 2002, when I joined STS *Stavros S. Niarchos* as 'Extra 2nd Officer' serving with Captain Barbara Campbell (Valetta to Málaga). Captain Barbara finally signed off my training record of 46 specific brig-related tasks. These tasks were all designed to assist and inform my competence as OOW in square-rigged vessels. The training was excellent, aided by the excellent people with whom I trained, including some highly skilled engineers, boatswains, cooks and deck hands. Plus, some very skilled voyage crews.

Finally, there follows a matrix of my voyages in my square-rigged ships between 2000 and 2017. I have used the year 2015 throughout my account so far, and, indeed, I retired in 2015. However, in 2017 I led a sea-party of 6th Form students from Broadway Academy, Birmingham – sailing as voyage crew in *Lord Nelson*.

Year	Square Rigged	Sea Area	Crew	Comments
2000	*Stav Niarchos*	South Coast	Mixed Adult	Training
2002	*Prince William*	Solent	Mixed Adult	Training
2002	*Prince William*	Sweden – UK	Mixed Adult	Training
2002	*Stav Niarchos*	Malta – Med	Mixed Adult	Extra OOW
2002	*Prince William*	North Sea	Mixed Adult	Navigator
2002	*Stav Niarchos*	UK Coastal	Mixed Youth	Navigator
2002	*Stav Niarchos*	UK – Atlantic	Mixed Adult	Navigator
2005	*Stav Niarchos*	Italian Med	Mixed Youth	Seaman OOW
2006	*Stav Niarchos*	Atlantic – Gib	Mixed Youth	Seaman OOW
2006	*Stav Niarchos*	Italian Med	Mixed Youth	Navigator
2007	*Prince William*	Azores	Mixed Youth	Seaman OOW
2008	*Lord Nelson*	UK Coastal	Mixed Adult	Seaman OOW
2009	*Tenacious*	UK – Irish Sea	Delivery ROI	Seaman OOW
2010	*Lord Nelson*	UK Coastal	Mixed Adult	Seaman OOW
2010	*Lord Nelson*	UK – Thames	UK Guides	Navigator
2010	*Lord Nelson*	UK – Clydeside	UK Guides	Seaman OOW
2010	*Stav Niarchos*	Tenerife Winter	Christmas	Seaman OOW
2011	*Stav Niarchos*	Canary – Azores	Delivery	Navigator
2011	*Pelican (Of Lon)*	Tall Ships Race	Mixed Youth	Navigator
2011	*Stav Niarchos*	UK Coastal	Mixed Adult	Navigator
2012	*Stav Niarchos*	Tenerife	Mixed Youth	Navigator
2012	*Stav Niarchos*	Winter Azores	Delivery UK	Navigator
2012	*Stav Niarchos*	North Sea	Mixed Youth	Navigator
2013	*Stav Niarchos*	UK Coastal	Mixed Youth	Seaman OOW
2013	*Stav Niarchos*	UK Coastal	Mixed Adult	Seaman OOW
2013	*Stav Niarchos*	Solent – UK	Mixed Adult	Seaman OOW
2014	*Stav Niarchos*	UK Coastal	Mixed Adult	Navigator
2015	*Stav Niarchos*	UK Coastal	Mixed Youth	Navigator
2017	*Lord Nelson*	Canary Islands	Mixed Youth	Voyage Crew

Author: Lord Nelson Navigator, 2010.

Each of my voyages listed above, in the largest of our historical UK square-rigged vessels, represents, for me, a remarkable 21st Century adventure at sea. But what will remain for my grandchildren's generation, given the current high costs? Sail training is worthwhile. It is about teamwork and a demanding social experience.

For me, as a lifetime seafarer, my sail training days have all been very rewarding. The sheer joy of returning under sail to the UK from the Azores, driven by south west winds day after day was amazing. We sailed in the steps of hard-nosed seafarers from past generations, as we embraced the Western Approaches. By 2022, most of my UK sail training ships listed above had gone. The end of an era in the UK? The emphasis today appears to favour much smaller vessels with lower running costs, and the ability to visit many UK anchorages and harbours. Square-rigged provision for UK Sea Cadets should remain; *JST* and *Tenacious* will hopefully survive after the Covid years. Sail Training International still lists worldwide sail training vessels. So there should remain the opportunity for UK youth to embark on adventure voyages. A computer generation needs the challenge of the sea.

Therefore, I will leave the final endorsement of sail training in the good hands of respected sailor, Sir Robin Knox-Johnston, and the late Duke of Edinburgh – as a decorated Royal Navy officer. Both commented in the year 2000 as *Stavros S.*

Niarchos was handed over to the STA by Appledore Shipbuilders. Sir Robin, at the time, was President of the Sail Training Association, and wrote after making an early voyage in SSN:

> *The essence of good seamanship is safety. The sea can be dangerous and must always be respected for its awesome power… the Sail Training Association can ensure that a voyage will be safe and challenging. The mission is personal development through the medium of Tall Ships… challenging young people to take on tasks they thought beyond them.*

HRH the late Prince Philip, Duke of Edinburgh KG, in his former role as Patron of the STA added,

> *The Sail Training Association is dedicated to the personal development of youth… the aim is to help young people learn about themselves, their capabilities and awareness of others in the exciting and demanding environment of a Tall Ship on the unpredictable sea. This unique challenge is an excellent preparation for life.*

This written comment was made by HRH Prince Philip as *Stavros S. Niarchos* entered service in 2000 with her UK Maiden Voyage.

It was my privilege to have served my time at sea; all voyages were completed during the reign of Her Late Majesty Queen Elizabeth II. I ended my professional service in my 70th year – and then trained for Witness Service at Crown Court.

As we began: 'They that go down to the sea in ships…in great waters… see the works of the Lord, and His wonders in the deep…' Psalm 107 vs. 23-24.

Epilogue Bravo

Award-Winning 2015 Merchant Navy War Poet

Sir Galahad and Welsh Guards 1982 – A Falklands Lament
Like other ships their time began in crane-commanding shipyard
Steel sinews soaring to a portent autumn sky.
Their names recalling legends of the bold.
With grim outpouring of events — both ships deploying south
To wrestle with familial strength the old
And bitter enemy called war.
These noble knights: deep-sea enduring Galahad and Tristram
Loyal knights and servants of the worthy RFA
Each ship manned by salt-encrusted Merchant Navy crowd.
Sir Galahad to face destructive wounds in daylight raid
And grasp in death the brutal South Atlantic shroud.

In Welsh Guard Principality, young men faced scrum and line-out
Facing thumping rugby games and time-out
With their fresh-faced brothers — long before
The ancient call to serve came flooding home.
Fast forward now to fateful 8th of June in Fitzroy Roads
Low-flying enemy Skyhawks coming in
Some troops were moved to wager on the odds.
Bombs pound auxiliary knights with vengeful joy —
Engulfing anchored Galahad;
Exposed troop-heavy Galahad.
That daylight billet for the Welsh Guard boy.
No hiding place. Black smoke consumes both lung and eye.
Heroic deeds abound. Ashore they hear the wounded cry.
While high above — the vapour trails from guardian Harriers
Leave crosses in the Bluff Cove sky.

Sea King and Wessex mercy missions brave
Fly blind above the burning grey-hulled ships.
Sir Tristram's quickly lowered boats

With life-rafts from Sir Galahad — spew
Welsh Guards — now brothers in adversity
To thrash in ice-cold sea; then land upon the rocky beach.
While film crew captures limbless scenes
To place on worldwide TV screens
The blood-stained Fitzroy foreshore — for some forever out of reach.
When devastating war is done
'Rejoice' our home-spun Siren cries
While mortal wounds of Galahad —
Bring endless tears to Cymru eyes.
Peter John Hill, 2015.

The bombed and charred hull of RFA *Sir Galahad* lay at her anchorage in the days following her attack by enemy Sky Hawks on 8th June 1982. RFA *Sir Tristram* was also hit. The attack and the heroic rescue of *Sir Galahad*'s surviving ship's company, was witnessed by ITN reporter the late Michael Nicholson. His moving account of heroism can be found in *Forgotten Voices of the Falklands*,

Sir Galahad, June 1982: Bombing.

McManners, H (Ebury Press, 2007). *Sir Galahad*'s OIC, Captain Phillip Roberts, was the last to leave his burning ship on the day of the 1982 attack.

Postscript

Evening Hymn

By Land and Sea. A sure and steadfast anchor for the soul.
Based on 'The Good Samaritan': Luke Chapter 10
Life-affirming mercy of heaven – Love of God beyond compare
Light of the World: From Bethlehem to Calvary illuminating
The Grace of God; His kindness to total strangers. By parable now declare.
He discovers us, bruised and broken on our lonely road to Jericho.
Beyond a poet's pen – to explore incarnate mystery.
The Father's heart revealed. The Everlasting Word: He steps into our history.
This Man – our Saviour Jesus Christ: His footprint from another place.
Emmanuel: God with us – He joins the arrow of our time and space.
Grace and Truth define His coming: Messiah – the Anointed One.
Breaking down barriers; scaling the ramparts of our proud disgrace.
Man of sorrows. Acquainted with tears shed by the human race.
Familiar with suffering. At Calvary abandoned. God's anointed,
Forsaken on a cross – at a time and place appointed.
Wounds that heal. Sweet sound. Amazing Grace.
He is our stronghold now – the Father's Son; our Kinsman Redeemer.
He raised us from the bruising wayside rocks,
From oppressive ambush and defeat; from the harsh reality
Of our ego-journey through our self-made wilderness.
Behold His loving kindness, now anointing us with oil and wine;
We are sheltered from the storm. In our place He stands.
Son of God: with dignity He endures our mockery. Observe His nail-pierced hands.
And the crown of thorns. Cruel deeds reflect the darkness of His Cross.
Yet He triumphs: The Word made flesh; Lamb of God; Bright Morning Star.
By faith we find His sheltered anchorage – beneath Eternal Wings.
His empty tomb. The light and hope that Easter brings.
Through God's own loving-kindness, redemption ground is now secured.
Not that we loved God; but He loved us. Therefore, worldwide voices join a song
Of tender mercy. These wounded lives have been restored.
Peter John Hill, Christmas 2021.

References

Writers can inspire and teach…

Conrad, J., *The Mirror of the Sea & A Personal Record.* (OUP, 1988).
Conrad, J., *Youth: A Narrative.* (Penguin, 1975).
Conrad, J., *Typhoon.* (Penguin, 1903).
Dana, R.H., *Two Years Before the Mast.* (JM Dent & Sons, 1978).
Daniels Jr, E.H., 'Eagle Seamanship'. *Naval Institute Press*, Annapolis, USA. (1990).
David, Shepherd and King., 'Psalm 21' and 'Psalm 139'. *Book of Psalms.*
Dear, I, Kemp, P., *The Pocket Oxford Guide to Sailing Terms.* (OUP, 1987).
Erikson, E., *Childhood and Society.* (Paladin, 1950).
Fontana, D., *Psychology for Teachers.* (Macmillan, 1982).
Goleman, D., *Emotional Intelligence.* (Bloomsbury, 1996).
Larkin., *Oxford Book 20th Century Verse.* (OUP, 1973).
Moore, D.A., *Basic Principles of Marine Navigation.* (Stanford Maritime, 1964).
Paul, aka Saul of Tarsus., 'Pauls Letter to the Colossians'. *New Testament.* (AD 60/61).
Peters, R.S., *Psychology and Ethical Development.* (George Allen & Unwin, 1974).
Robins, N., *Manchester Liners: An Extraordinary Story.* (Bernard McCall, 2011).
Robinson, D.M., *Munro's Maths for Deck Officers.* (Brown Son & Ferguson, 2020).
Slocum, J., *Sailing Alone Around the World.* (NY: Sheridan House Inc., 1899).
Sobel, D., *Longitude.* (London: Fourth Estate, 1996).
Warner, P., Lock Keeper's Daughter. (Brewin Books, 1986).

Further Reading: Joseph Conrad is always a good start, but his writing, at times, can be as deep as the ocean. My early voyages taught me to respect the stormy sea; but, under sail I began to understand people. The ocean will continue to offer a real challenge to my grandchildren's generation and to the generations that follow them, if they are prepared to venture beyond mobile phone range. We all need to observe our own mid-ocean albatross, and feel for ourselves the wind of freedom beneath our fragile human wings. But beware, the sea remains implacable. Conrad warns us to respect its power, but never to love the sea… 'The ocean has no compassion, no faith, no law, no memory'.
Peter John Hill – on the eve of my 77th birthday, (21st March 2023).

Also published by Brewin Books

From Africa to the Arctic (HMS Beagle)
Peter Ward
ISBN: 978-1-85858-237-5
Price: £6.95

From Stormy Seas to Calmer Waters
Commander Anthony Pearse
ISBN: 978-1-85858-427-0
Price: £7.95

Hospital Ship (HMHS Tjitjalengka)
Jack Woolman
ISBN: 978-1-85858-197-2
Price: £8.95

My Incredible Journey – From Cadet to Command
Rear Admiral Peter Dingemans CB DSO
ISBN: 978-1-85858-559-8
Price: £14.95

Pacific Voyage (HMS Arbiter)
Peter Ward
ISBN: 978-1-85858-276-4
Price: £9.95

Proceed As Requisite – The Exploits of a WWI Submariner
Geoffrey C. West
ISBN: 978-1-85858-519-2
Price: £8.95

Wet and Dry – The Memoirs of a Naval Officer
Commander Geoffrey Greenish
ISBN: 978-1-85858-479-9
Price: £9.95

All available to purchase at www.brewinbooks.com